©Steve Marchal—PP®F

COME AND WRESTLE:
DESIGNER VS. FOREIGN TYPEFACE

Issue
55

AD
Art Director
CD
Creative Director
D
Designer
P
Photographer
DS
Design Studio

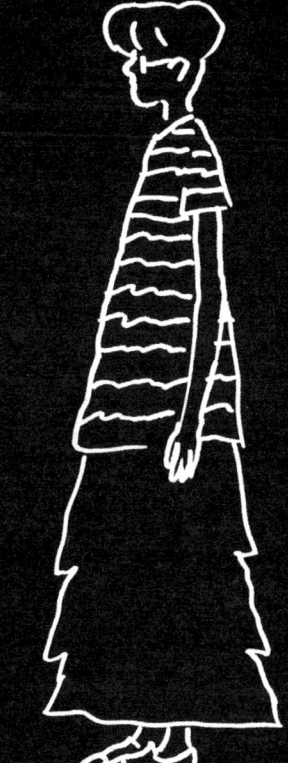

Nicole Lo
Editor-in-Chief

COME AND WRESTLE ROUND 2

Recently, the Internet has been buzzing with articles about the development trend of foreign typeface design. After the publication of *BranD* Issue 54 whose theme is *Come and Wrestle: Designer vs. Hanzi*, we came up with the idea to have interviews with designers from different cities around the world based on our extensive research and new understanding on foreign typefaces for the layout of magazine. We learned that type design is challenging no matter in which script through the detailed and meticulous responses of interviewees, and there is always a story about type design behind the design. Designer needs to take various problems into consideration during the type design process. Each effort is like an attack. Perseverance is the most basic principle for designer no matter the project is simple or complicated, so I think that type design presents a sportsmanship. Designer seems to shout "Come and wrestle, typeface!" when he or she designs Hanzi or foreign typeface. If there was a judo tournament between designer and foreign typeface, I think we would play the role of cheerleaders!

Please turn the page if you want to improve the level of type design knowledge. Hopefully this issue can provide you with the latest trend of foreign typeface.

PRELIMINARY

FURTHER

PROFICIENCY

ADVANCED COMPRE

MASTERY OF

PROFESSION

1

008

015

Learning is never something that can be mastered in a short duration of time, no matter if the field in question is type design or judo. At the beginning stage of learning type design, designers need to pay attention to the most minute details, such as the nuances between different typefaces on the keys of typewriters. Typewriters manufactured in different eras invariably bear the cultural imprints of that age with the influence of specific history, society and culture. A small letter on a typewriter is like a totem of its time. Comparatively speaking, in the field of judo, there is a strict kyu and dan ranking system, which is concretely demonstrated in the changes of belt color as the judokas' ranking rise. After novices learn the basic techniques of judo and begin to move forward in their judo level towards the higher grades, they need to observe the most intricate and minute details behind each judo movement and technique.

BEAUTY OF HUMANITY HIDDEN IN A MACHINE

Editor
Gakky Luk

Retro items like film cameras and pixel fonts are making a comeback. They bring the trends of the 20th century back to life again. To create a retro atmosphere, some owners of vintage stores decorate their interiors with nostalgic, retro ornaments like painted dial telephones, rusting iron gates with carved patterns, or typewriters.

Speaking of such typewriters, you may have seen such items in a number of movies or television series. In *Populaire*, the stylish Rose pulls back her hair and moves her fingers quickly on the keys of the typewriter. In *Love Actually*, Jamie, a casually dressed writer, sits in a pavilion by the lake, stopping to think from time to time, and records his fleeting bursts of inspiration on his typewriter. In *House of Cards*, when Frank Underwood uses his Underwood Typewriter, it suddenly reminds him of what his father said: "This Underwood built an empire, now you go and build one of your own." No matter it is a short close-up in the movie, or the background sound changing from slow to fast gradually, or an ornament being laid aside, nowadays typewriters seem very far from people's modern lives. Perhaps many young people do not realize that the humble typewriter was once responsible for a complete revolution in the way of writing.

In the middle of the 19th Century, the rapid development of commercial communications led to a growing demand for writing machines. In 1865, Rasmus Malling Hansen, the principal at the Royal Institute for the Deaf, invented the Hansen Writing Ball. The writing ball went into production in 1870, and it became the first commercially produced typewriter. The Hansen Writing Ball is an ergonomic innovation. Its distinctive feature is an arrangement of 52 keys on a large brass hemisphere, which looks like an oversized pincushion.

1865
HANSEN WRITING BALL

1

The influential Sholes and Glidden typewriter was patented in 1868. After its invention, people started to use the word "typewriter" to refer to the machine used for this purpose.

The typewriter was a co-invention of Christopher Latham Sholes, Carlos Glidden and Samuel W. Soule. Their first typewriter model had a keyboard made of black and white keys, leading *Scientific American* to describe it as a "literary piano".

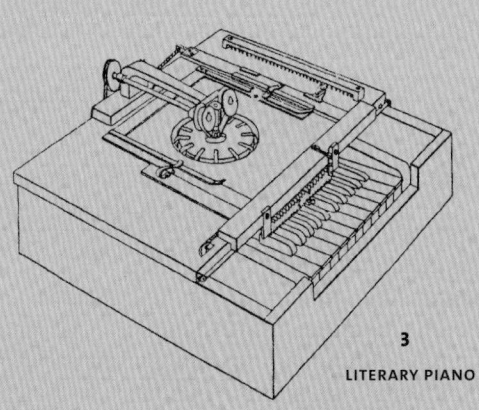

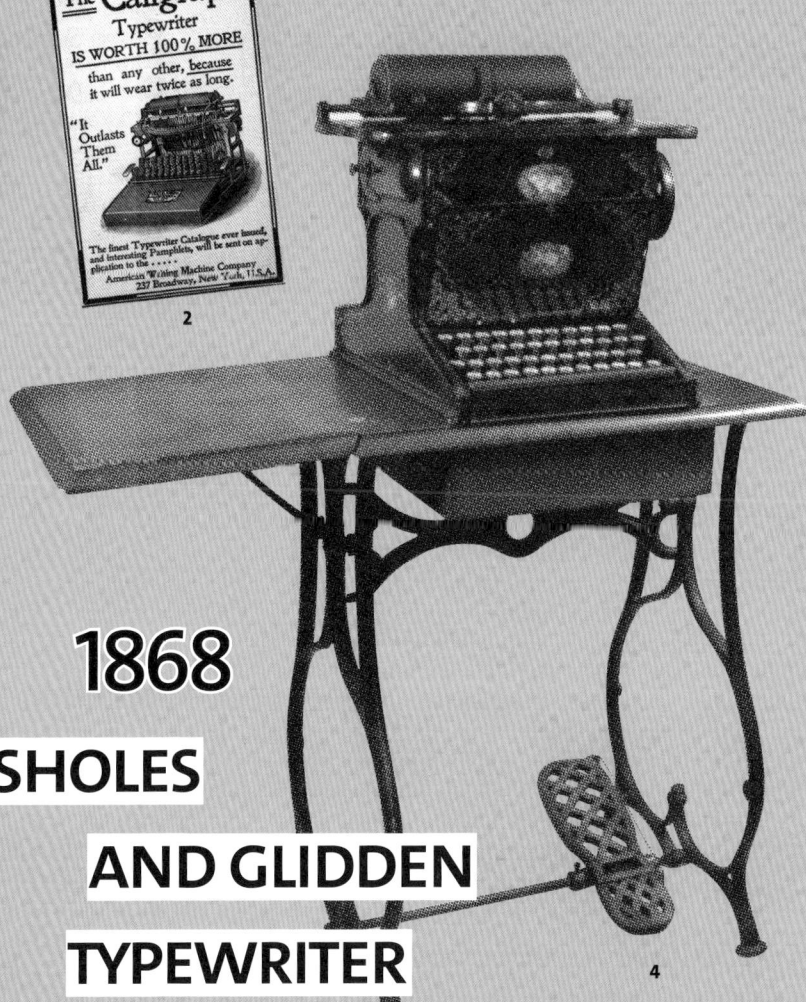

2

1868
SHOLES AND GLIDDEN TYPEWRITER

3

LITERARY PIANO

4

The influence exerted by the Sholes and Glidden typewriter laid not only in the naming of this typing machine, but also in finalizing the order of the keys, which persists with our own modern electronic keyboards. After getting the patent, Sholes continued to improve and upgrade the typewriter. Previously, the keys of the typewriter were arranged in alphabetical order. The 26 letters were tightly spaced to ensure all of them would fit in the same position when people type. However, some adjacent letter pairs would often clash with each other when used successively at high speed, leading to a slowdown in typing speed.

QWERTY KEYBOARD

Image Courtesy of Stack Overflow

The QWERTY Keyboard Designed by Sholes

To solve this problem, Sholes separated the most commonly used letter pairs out and placed each of them as much as possible in opposite positions, so as to solve the problem caused by jamming keys. This QWERTY design worked effectively, which is why it continues to be applied in the modern keyboards. The first commercial typewriter with this design was introduced to the market in 1874, the first time the public came in contact with the QWERTY keyboard.

When the digital age dawned, although electronic keyboards connected to computers no longer had any issues with jamming keys, enterprises like IBM and Mircrosoft insisted on keeping the QWERTY layout for keyboards, giving people a smooth and pleasing transition from the age of the mechanical typewriter to the present computer era.

QWERTY KEYBOARD
Image Courtesy of David Spencer

YELLOW BELT – PRELIMINARY PREPARATION

6

1880s
INDEX TYPEWRITER

The index typewriter, which came onto the market in the 1880s, gained popularity because of its miniature size and portability. Index typewriters were initially popular in a niche market, with travelers being a particular target customer because of its features. The way to operate the index typewriter is to select the character on a dial or index, strike the pointer or stylus, then the chosen character can be printed on the paper. People can skip the step of trying to learn the layout of keyboard and can type directly because there is no keyboard structure in this kind of typewriter. Compared with traditional mechanical typewriters, its simple structure and relatively low price made it popular with many customers.

In addition, index typewriters can be adapted to various scripts, such as Chinese and Japanese, both of which contain thousands of characters. In the middle of the 20th Century, the Chinese writer Yutang Lin applied the principle of the index typewriter to invent the MING KWAI typewriter.

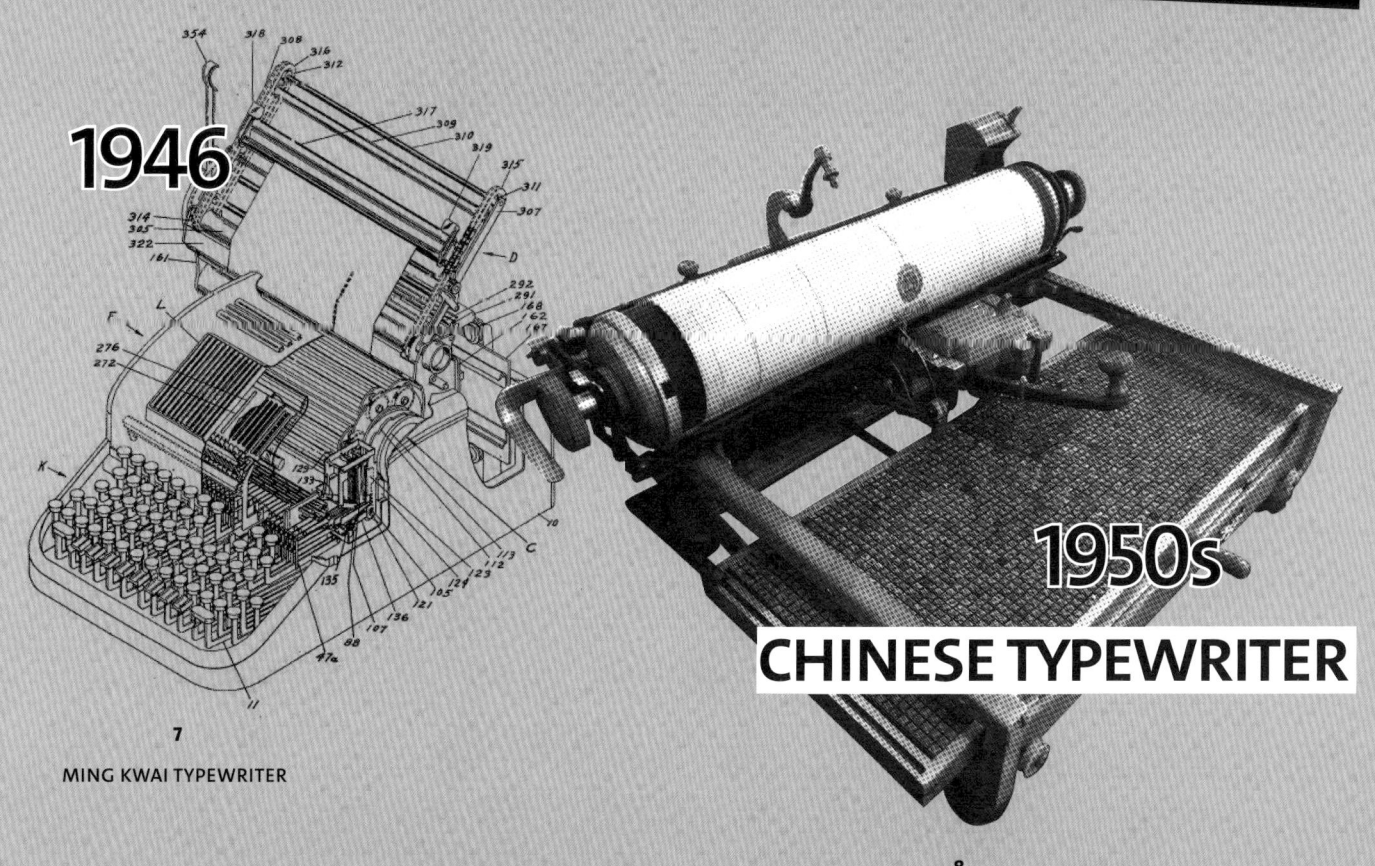

1946

1950s
CHINESE TYPEWRITER

7

MING KWAI TYPEWRITER

8

Besides more visible typewriter design elements like shape, structure, and arrangement of the keyboard, the characters on the keys of the typewriter are also well worth noting. Because of mechanical restrictions, when a typist pressed a key, the platen would automatically move forward the same distance so going back and revising was kept simple. Therefore, the typeface on the document produced by a typewriter in the early days was always monospaced font, which, to a certain extent, cannot provide a really fluent and pleasing reading experience. In 1957, Olivetti S.p.A., an Italian information technology company, began inventing and producing the Olivetti Graphika, a typewriter that could type out proportional font. The width of each type mould was adjusted according to the width of the letter. For example, some lower-case letters such as *i*, *l* and *j* were shrunk in width, while *w* and *m* were widened. This adjustment helped to improve the legibility of the text. Notably, Olivetti Graphika was the first typewriter that allowed people to manually manipulate the letter spacing.

1957
OLIVETTI GRAPHIKA

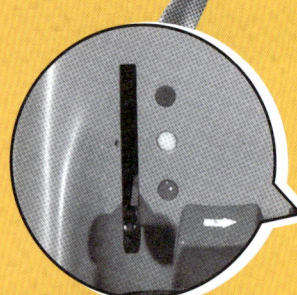

9

As technology developed, IBM introduced the Selectric typewriter in 1961, which, with the Electronic Brother typewriter, made it possible to offer different letter spacing on the same typewriter.

FONT BALL

11

1961
SELECTRIC TYPEWRITER

10

Today, of course, adjusting the letter spacing on computer screen can be achieved with one simple click.

BROTHER TYPEWRITER

12

Today on electronic devices, if people want to change font size, they can simply select from the font size drop-down list, or even directly input the numerical value of the font size they want. However, in the era of the typewriter, due to objective factors like the shortage of material and technical limitations, people didn't have many choices in terms of font size. The commonly used font sizes were pica and elite.

The acronym CPI stands for characters per inch. It is a measure of the number of typographic characters that fits into a one-inch space. 1 pica means 10 characters per inch, which basically translates to the font size we know as 12pt today, and 1 elite means 12 characters per inch, which is equal to 10pt today.

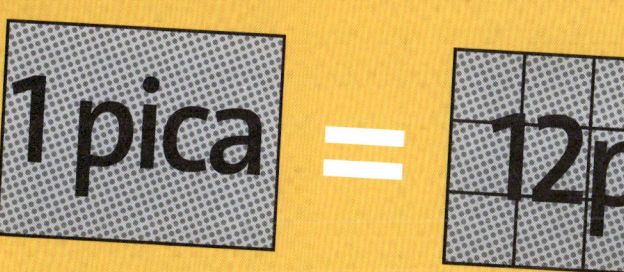

Tapping the keys of a typewriter with fingers, seeing the keys hit the type mould on the ribbon and finally seeing the ink trace of characters left on the paper. These actions endow the printing process, as achieved with a mechanical typewriter, with a touch of humanistic beauty. Typewriter fonts bring people this nostalgic, retro and distinctive feeling. The period between the 1950s and 1960s was the time that computers assumed greater and greater importance. IBM designed a series of typefaces suitable for computers based on typewriter fonts: serif fonts like Courier, and sans-serif fonts like Letter Gothic and Orator.

The mechanical beauty of the typewriter is reflected in its sophisticated design. People can hear the clicking sound when the type mould clicks on the ribbon, the tinkling bell sound when a line is finished and shifts to the next line automatically, or the rustling sound of the platen roll after the carriage return is pressed. As people record their feelings on paper using a typewriter, the sound it makes is as if one is playing a visible tangible tune on a piano. When people touch the letters, the unique feeling of the uneven paper endows the document with a deeper meaning.

1-12   Image Courtesy of Wikimedia Commons

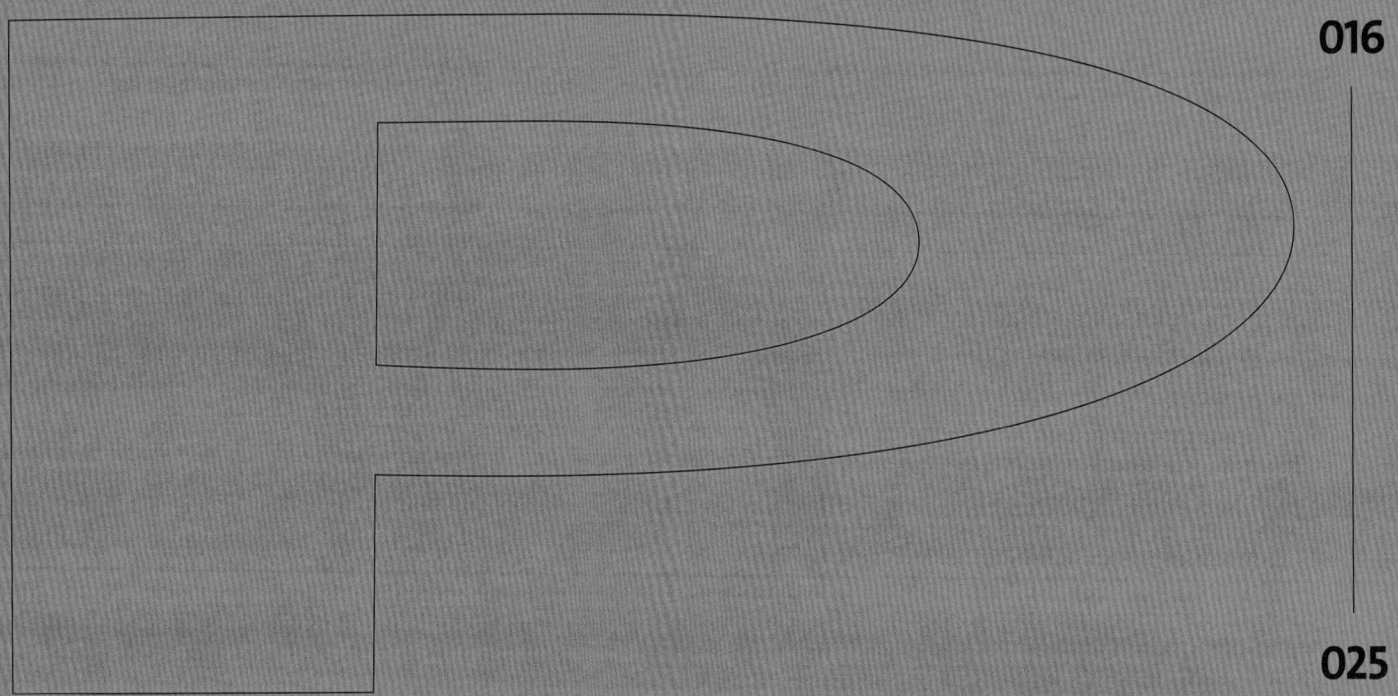

Type designers need to have a clear understanding of the rationale behind each step in the design process. Based on extensive research, Japanese type designer Toshi Omagari has systematically explored the reasons behind the emergence and popularity of pixel fonts, as well as the difficulties that need to be tackled in each case. For judokas who have gained yellow belt, the orange belt is their next target. To achieve the orange belt, judokas need to gradually develop a higher level of awareness and understanding of how each judo technique can be carried out in a distinctive way. Within the process which involves extremely intense observation, judokas can often establish a highly systematic way of thinking.

THE INFINITE POSSIBILITIES OF THE 8×8 PIXEL GRID

Editor
Gakky Luk

Cars flow by on the traffic-clogged roads, piles of emails and messages flood into people's computers, and the lights in office buildings lit up brightly into the darkness of the night. It seems the relentless pace of modern life is gradually and inexorably driving people into a corner. When people finally find a moment to catch their breath, they gradually transfer their social life from real life to online world. Mobile games have become a huge part of people's social lives in recent years. In addition to the tension of the game playing, the vivid scenery and the gripping background sound, the typeface used in games is also an important factor. A suitably chosen typeface for a game can help players to grasp the game situation instantly, which can greatly enhance the playing experience. Typeface is to the game as air is to people—it makes no sound and is hardly noticed, yet it is indispensable. As Toshi Omagari said: "Being unnoticed is what typography is supposed to do."

Toshi Omagari, a senior type designer, delves into the typefaces used in the popular or niche arcade games between the 1970s and 1990s. Based on his research, he wrote a book called *Arcade Game Typography*. As type design technology for arcade games was quite primitive at that time, type designers had to use the 8×8 pixel grid, which undoubtedly made great challenges in terms of spacing, structure and color. Looking back at the pixel fonts of that time from today's perspective, those works have become iconic symbols of that era.

Omagari once worked for Monotype as a type designer. He is an expert in the field of multilingual type design. He has the ability to adjust his thinking swiftly depending on different contexts in his pursuit of providing a unique vision for his type designs. Also, Omagari gives full play to his design strengths. He has participated in the Google project to develop Mongolian typeface of Noto fonts as well as the Marco font family which includes Latin, Cyrillic and Mongolian.

吃豆人 PAC-MAN NAMCO/1980

《吃豆人》的字体基本上和《弹珠台砖块》(见第20页)相同，不过Y是对称造型。当记录字体在不同时间中的发展时，必须严肃对待这样的细节。《吃豆人》是一个尤其重要的案例。

它使用了雅达利字体最广泛使用的变体，这种变体主要被南梦宫使用，但也由于这款游戏的流行被使用在了其他地方。《铲子骑士》(Shovel Knight, Yacht Club Games, 2014)

凤凰之子 SON OF PHOENIX ASSOCIATED OVERSEAS MFR, INC/1985

《凤凰之子》的字体大量使用45°的笔画，字母底部的图形也都处理成了方角。这款字体具有一种机械感和未来感，但并不完全连贯。在这里加入这款字体的真正原因是为了展示游戏中令人愉悦的开篇。与著名的"All your base…"(见第11页)不同，"Yuppies, hamburgers and mom"这个短语并非出于糟糕的英语翻译——它在日语中也没有任何意义。

01 SANS REGULAR

雅达利字体解析 ANATOMY OF THE ATARI FONT

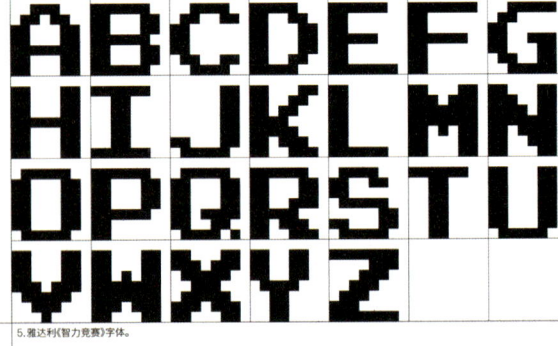

5. 雅达利《智力竞赛》字体。

6. 直线解读。

7. 曲线解读。

8. 折中解读。

一款游戏的全部字符 ALL CHARACTERS IN A GAME

8×8字体只是街机游戏字体排印中的一小部分,且仅在这部分中,本书中也有有明显的缺漏,例如基于比例宽度和矢量图形的系统。即使是本书涉及到的游戏,通常也不止包含一款 8×8 字体,还会有其他字体和美术字样式的支持。在这里,我们分析两款游戏,以及其中的每一个字符。

BLOCKADE
Gremlin/1976

早期的街机游戏没有排行榜,因为存储器中的每一比特空间都很珍贵。在这款早期的《贪食蛇》游戏中,图像数据极少以至于不能算作一款字体——一个 "GAME OVER" 字符,数字 0 到 9,仅此而已。其他的图像数据则与文字无关,实心的空心方头用于区分两位玩家,砖块用于标示游戏区边界,以及蛇的轨迹,半透网格会在玩家撞击障碍物的地方闪烁来指示死亡。

1. 玩家1和玩家2的蛇头。
2. 数字用于指示游戏轮次和胜利数。
3. 预制的 "GAME OVER" 字标,在游戏中作为整体出现。
4. 在玩家撞击处闪烁的单元。

OUT RUN
Sega/1986

《超越》是 1986 年最好看的游戏之一。玩家驾驶一辆比拉利 Testarossa 穿行在各种欧洲风光之中,机柜的头枕式扬声器系统播放着优美的游戏音乐。游戏由铃木裕 (Yu Suzuki) 设计,而他在前一年制作了《太空哈利》。8×8 字体原本为《太空哈利》(见第30页) 设计的,但这款游戏中的字母 V 得到了修正。字体包含灰色、绿色和粉红色色板。这款字体还有一个更小的版本,但是没有在游戏中使用。

8×16 的字体被用在排行榜和姓名键入处,显示为黄色、黑色、柠檬黄——蓝色、柠檬黄——黑色和红色——黑色的色板。速度计使用了另一套 8×16 的数字字体。此外,还有游戏标题字和其他杂项图像素材,例如 "INSERT COINS!",它由特制的美术字组成,而由有制作成此其他字符。

从未使用的图像素材来看,游戏的渊源显而易见。游戏代码中隐藏了 "@SEGA 1985" 的标识,以及同样很酷的 16×16 方块字体,该款字体也使用于《太空哈利》中,来宣告下一场场景。哈利《太空哈利》中的玩家角色)的图标也包含在内。

6. 游戏标题字。
7. 从《太空哈利》中遗留下来的图像素材。
8. 《超越》的屏幕元素。
9. 速度计字体以及用于选择歌曲的音效。
10. 似乎未被使用的图像资产。
11. 在玩家按到达检查点时出现。
12. "吸引模式" 下出现的投币提示。
13. 右下角的场景指示。
14. 歌曲选择画面,高分榜画面以及剩余时间所使用的 8×16 像素字体。
15. 原设计用于《太空哈利》的 8×8 像素字。

RALLY BIKE DASH YAROU TOAPLAN/TAITO/1988

一款俯视角的竞速游戏。这里展示的字体未被使用。这很令人遗憾,因为为尽管其中的字体自有其魅力,但远远不如这一款。这是一个带有深度三维效果的、厚实的块状设计,其中的内部空间则采用了斜对角线。H和W之间的字区别在于中间块的高度。游戏数据中没有出现K。

BIO-SHIP PALADIN UPL/1990

一款横版飞行射击游戏,玩家可以移动自己的飞船,并且用带有目标十字线瞄准;或锁定在一个位置,向屏幕上的任意方向射击。这款游戏的字体带有一种三维浮雕效果,其边界模糊,以至于很难从基础字形中分离出来。这是一款独特的字体,能够根据你看它的方式而显得更细。

GHOX TOAPLAN/1991

一款《快打砖块》(Arkanoid) 的翻版,玩家可以前后移动,这是同类游戏中并不常见的特性。游戏中的字体具有令人印象深刻的纹理细节,并且由于中部的深色像素,垂直字干显得向内凹陷,类似赫尔曼·查普夫 (Hermann Zapf) 1958年的字体 "Optima"。字干的粗度可以更一致些。

GUARDIANS OF THE 'HOOD ATARI GAMES/1992

在这款横版格斗游戏中,玩家扮演一名安保人员,负责一个有报酬问题的社区治安,虽然游戏的主要字体是《狂暴弹珠》(见第27页) 版的《智力竞赛》字体 (见第18页和44-45页),但在角色介绍中使用了另一种字体,它看起来像是字母 I 变形金属上,这种字形较为罕见,也无法从背景中分离出来。

RIOT NMK/1992

这是一款难度极高的游戏,在游戏中你需要同一支能够以数量优势吓开天的军队战斗。其主要字体也是一款罗马体,此处展示的字体其次,出现在高分榜上。由于具有笔记本外形,因此它的背景颜色和下划线也是设计的一部分。

REBUS MICROHARD/1995

一款由意大利开发商 Microhard 制造的酒吧问答机。与该公司的所有街机游戏一样,这款游戏也包含情色内容。这款字体也用在了 Microhard 的其他游戏中,不过B是翻转的。那些中间弯曲的字母在字距上不会出现问题 (见 C、D、E和F),但字母间常有时会相像。这种上色方式背后的意图不明确,但看起来确实很酷。

01 SANS REGULAR

After years of research, the Chinese version of *Arcade Game Typography* written by you has finally been released in China. What difficulties have you met in your research for this book? In which media would you like the book to be quoted?

During the few years of writing the book, I spent every night and weekend on research. The subject I chose, namely arcade games, was quite vast and demanded a lot of digging and organizing. I had to be smart about this, made note of everything in one big spreadsheet, and made everything into a functional color font by using Python. The following part was the writing which was equally demanding. I have written a dissertation for my master's degree in Britain and I had thought I would never write at such length again, yet here I was re-living the same torture. But this time it was a bit more pleasurable. Looking back, the project had no shortage of difficulties but I absolutely loved it as I knew that it would be a wonderful book in the end and the first of its kind. As for which media I would like the book to be quoted in, there is no better place than video games. I think I will be able to spot the influence of the book in the games especially when I see more color fonts being used.

We often encounter trouble with font combining during typesetting, such as combining fonts in different scripts. When choosing typefaces, what details should be observed to make sure the typefaces in different scripts are perfectly matched? Someone said that there should not be more than 3 typefaces in a design. Do you follow any rules like that?

When matching fonts from multiple scripts, the details are less important. You need to prioritize the bigger picture stuff like general feeling of the typeface, x-height (or in more general terms, the size of "busy zones") and matching weights which is often overlooked. You'll most likely end with a pretty limited number of choices that meet those criteria, which is unfortunate, but it also would make the selection process easier. If you do not know whether the fonts at hand are good or not, you need to do more research on their source foundries. To answer the second question about the number of typefaces used for one project, I agree that more fonts equals less focus and three is usually enough, not counting the weights and equivalents in other languages.

Neue Plak

When you design typeface in different scripts, do you try to jump out of the limitations of the environment to design the typeface?

When I design typefaces in different scripts, it is usually within the context of corporate branding of my clients. Their interest is a unified voice throughout their business reach, and there is not much room for artistic whim to speak. In many cases, you can design each script in the same visual language, but not all the time. A casual Latin script is pretty difficult to translate to a non-Latin one, and you are sometimes forced to take more liberties and interpret it more loosely. When it comes to making purely artistic decisions about my non-native scripts, I make sure it has a solid reason, and more importantly, that it works. Breaking tradition is less welcome when outsiders do it, which is just the way it is. Even though I am not particularly afraid of being rejected, I do not want to be disrespectful.

If you want to share a story behind a typeface, which one would you choose?

I would like to talk about Albertus, a classic inscriptional typeface that is popular for titling. It was designed in the early 1930s by Berthold Wolpe, a Jewish German who immigrated to UK, and it was his first commercial typeface from Monotype (and I redesigned it as Albertus Nova). His son Paul told me that the rest of his family could not move over to the UK at the time. After Albertus became successful, Wolpe could spend the royalties earned from the typeface to take his families to UK before the WWII started. I like this story behind Albertus, not because of its gorgeous design, but because of the lives it saved.

Before starting to design a quality typeface, designers must accurately visualize the purpose of the design, the required visual characteristics, the relevant market trend of design, and also know how to select suitable solutions to achieve these objectives based on their existing knowledge. Similarly, each judo ranking has different standards for the judokas' technical and theoretical knowledge. When seeking the green belt, judokas need to accurately judge how and when to use each technique in each circumstance.

LOCALIZATION OF TYPE DESIGN

Editor
Gakky Luk

In recent years, ... us the field of type design, giving a chance to the domestic type ... ock itself to burst back to life. At the same time, type designers are ... gn in terms of future development. Due to technological and economic ... e become ubiquitous in all societies, and there is an emerging trend whereby ... re and more affordable for individuals. This has accelerated the emergence of a large ... studios often established by individuals or a handful of collaborators. ... orld, although some traditional large font foundries with huge font libraries can provide cus... atic one-stop services, some small-sized type design studios have found favor among clients because ... ty and high speed. In this issue, *BranD* seeks to explore this fascinating sector with a series of interviews ... type designers. Some represent local font foundries with long histories, some work in small self-design oriented ... dios, and some seek in their work to unite independent type designers from all over the world. Apart from ... e designers deal with the details of type design, *BranD* is also very keen to get their take on all sorts ... aced fonts and proportional fonts, how typeface style can be established, how distinctive client ... type design, creative innovations from static typeface to dynamic one and many more. ... designers and readers with a sight into how other scripts operate, a way to observe ... involved—from creative inspiration to achieving pragmatic balance—when ... e same time, *BranD* hopes these interviews can offer some insights into the de... ew Zealand, Northern Europe and other places, as we share with readers exci... ted type design industry practitioners.

JAGER DS/VJ-Type

Dialogue with WUJIN SIM

Wujin Sim

Sim works in education and publishing industry, and focuses on the design methodology of books and typefaces. He has been the director of Sandoll since 2017, and currently, the head of Sandoll Type Design Institute. Sandoll has a wide range of experiences of multi-language projects such as CJK font development and Korean-Latin matching. It has participated in global projects with corporations like Microsoft, Apple, Google, Adobe, etc.

Interviewer
Gakky Luk

GREEN BELT—PROFICIENCY IN TYPE DESIGN

BREAK THE LIMITATION OF MONOSPACE

Sandoll Jeongche

Sandoll LateSpring

Q&A

The size of Korean letters changes depending on the position. For example, in the Korean letters "하" and "한", the size of "ㅎ" and "ㅏ" is different. Are there any rules to standardize the size of Korean letters?

It's a very interesting question. It's a Korean linguistic term called Natja (낱자) in design, which means a single syllable. Each piece of letters combines and becomes a syllabic block. It's similar to the formation of Hanja (meaning "Hanzi"), forming characters with plural elements. As you mentioned, the sizes and the shapes of Natja are various. Moreover, for Chinese, Japanese and Korean (CJK) fonts, it's basic to fix the width of glyphs. What is more difficult to keep balance among each different Natja. Helmut Schmid, a graphic designer, described the Korean character as a prison. He once question how they can be put in the same sized spaces even though the shapes are diverse. In conclusion, there are no standard rules, because there are many variables, depending on the design. I think, however, it can be roughly divided into fixed and proportional widths. Maybe Korea is the most active nation among these three countries in terms of thinking about proportional widths. It's because we have to keep in mind the pursuit of harmony with the letters of other languages, which mostly have proportional widths. Korean graphic designers as well as type designers have a keen interest in harmonized typesetting with the letters of other languages. It might be a unique characteristic of Korean design.

The strokes and structures of Korean characters are relatively simple. What difficulties need to be overcome in the process of designing Korean typefaces?

The gap between the letters which have the most and the fewest strokes in Hangul (meaning "Korean alphabet") is smaller than Hanja, but bigger than Latin characters: the frequently used one with the fewest strokes (ㅡ) is written with 2 strokes, and the one with the most strokes (뻴) has 14 strokes. That's why it's both easy and difficult to keep the grayscale of letters. I feel it's ambiguous, as the gap is neither big nor small enough to pursue either similarity or dissimilarity in the greyscale among letters. So, we need to consider the proportional widths again, just like Latin letters. However, I can't say that the proportional widths are always better than the fixed ones, as the fixed widths have their own strength: even though we change the weight of letters, the length of the lines of writing are not changed. Sandoll chooses one of them depending on its uses, and tries to make font families which have both of them at the same time. It's similar to the trend that the modern Latin types support both proportional and fixed widths of numerals through the Opentype feature. Sandoll finds it hugely worthwhile to adjust the balances among not only Hangul, but Latin scripts, Chinese Hanzi, Japanese Kanji, Kana, and so on. It is very tough, but I find that it is interesting and engaging.

In recent years, Chinese designers have paid more and more attention to type design. Is it the same in Korea? How do you see the development of the Korean type industry these days?

I think it's a very significant tendency. One of the difficulties (which is also one of the great attractions) of type design is that it has to pursue things from both tradition and modernity at the same time. There are many things we can try to change in spite of the fact that there are so many things to be aware of, preserve and check carefully as the history of characters is very long. I mean, it's an area where we can make a range of attempts, ponder and make progress alone or with a small group of people. There has been a lot of work by independent designers over the last decade. The technical developments have played a vital role because it was hard to design a set of font alone in the past, as CJK fonts have a lot of glyphs. Sandoll is trying to foster a rich environment for type design—we offer the platform for type designers to sell their own typefaces, in order to support their economic independence.

하하하호호
방방방곡곡
땡땡땡땡
시시각각
조심조심

Sandoll Hoyoyo

프레스PRESS

Sandoll Press

Dialogue with VJ-TYPE

VJ-Type

VJ-Type designs custom fonts for the graphic design projects they work on. The team designs fonts like everything else they design: with their own artistic voice and sensibility. They clearly focus on drawing strong and unique fonts.

035   GREEN BELT — PROFICIENCY IN TYPE DESIGN

Interviewer
Gakky Luk

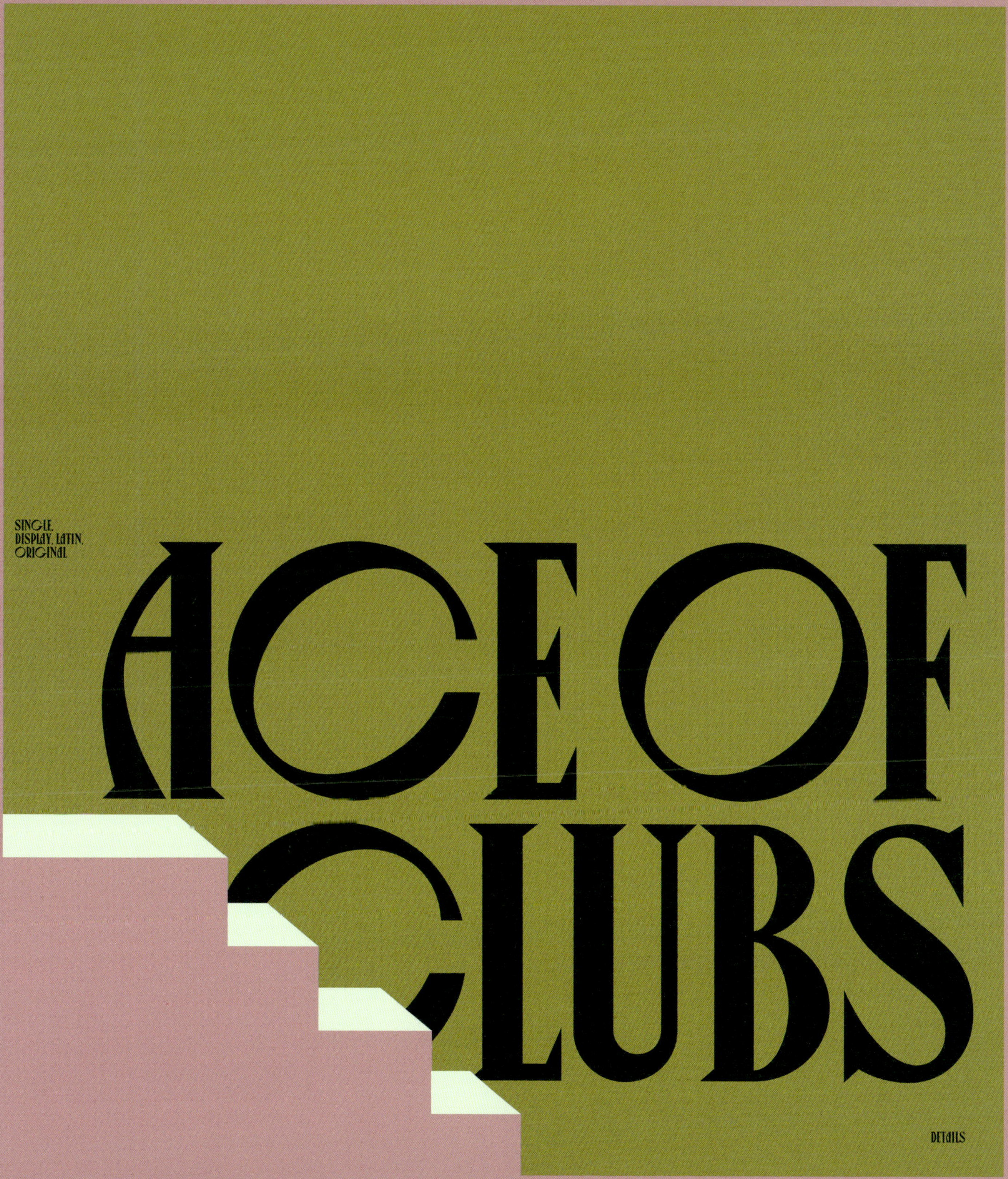

No Secrets in Design

SINGLE,
DISPLAY, LATIN,
ORIGINAL

ACE OF CLUBS

DETAILS

CANOPEE

CAKO TYPEFACE

VJ-Type has customized typefaces for various brands. What role do you believe typeface plays in design? Where did the inspiration for customized typefaces come from?

Font is almost the most important tool in graphic design. If you choose your typeface with care, you won't need many design tricks to make a project look good. Typefaces and colors are also the fundamental tools.

When we design a custom font, firstly, inspiration comes from the project itself. And of course, it is always driven by our own aesthetics and by historic references. It can be paintings, engravings, decorative objects, decor, and architectures.

Compared with traditional typeface, the typefaces you design have more personal characteristics. How can personality and legibility be balanced in type design?

We became type designers along the way. We didn't get any specific school education or training in type design. At first, our studio was a graphic design and illustration studio. This is why we say our typefaces are graphic designer's typefaces. Our fonts aren't highly technical, and we don't develop many styles for each font. We clearly focus on style. This way of doing type design comes from our graphic design work.

In addition to that, with our years of practice, we have developed a very personal style, a recognizable style, a kind of "Violaine & Jérémy" signature. This signature style can be described thus: our aesthetics is timeless with a modern twist.

Achieving balance between personality and legibility is something we focus on a lot, and the only way to achieve balance is by working many times on each letter. There is no secret—for us, work is the answer to everything.

What are the important aspects to a successful design of a customized typeface?

It really depends on which kind of font it is. If it's a display font, then we really focus on style and personality. Most of the time, our clients are just happy with what we present to them. But if it's a complete font family with many styles for a corporate identity, then the client we work with is really important. We like to think that a project is always the combination of what we want and what our clients want. This is not a selfish exercise; it is really important to discuss and think with the people who come to us with the task of designing their company's font.

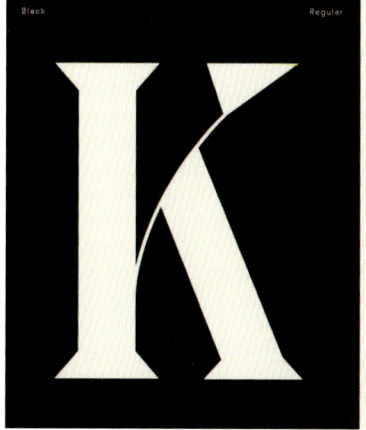

01 TERRE

Agriculture
Le défi est dans les champs — 14
Jean Viard — 18
Quelle sera verte ma cité ?
Aurélien Yol — 20
Plus d'IA, moins de chimie ?
Datarama — 22

Énergie
L'énergie toujours plus verte — 28
Alexis Landrieu — 31
Carburant renouvelable
Dominique Desjeux, Un problème media depuis 200 ans — 32
Datarama — 34

Transport
Les routes de la mobilité responsable — 38
Xavier Aymonod — 43
À la carte
Nathalie Ortar — 44
Bannir la voiture des villes ?
Datarama — 46

02 CORPS

Beauté
Se réinventer en beauté — 52
Jean-François Amadieu — 56
L'éternel standard féminin
Stanislas Vandier — 58
L'algorithme dans la peau
Datarama — 60

Sport
Des datas, des filles et des leds… — 64
Béatrice Barbusse — 68
Même pas mâle !
Pierre Mignot — 70
Le protocole thérapeutique
Datarama — 72

Habillement
Clean is the new chic ! — 76
Frédéric Godart — 80
Designer pour durer
Mylène L'Orguilloux — 82
Stopper les chutes
Datarama — 84

03 HABITAT & VILLE

Bâtiment
Philippe Starck, Geek ecology — 90
Les bâtisseurs du green — 98
Olivier Grange — 102
Un bois vraiment béton
Eric Cassar — 104
« Et - bim ! »
Datarama — 106

Immobilier
Un avant-goût de disruption — 110
Vincent Pavanello — 114
Opération accélération
Aurélien Gouttefarde — 116
Dessine-moi une proptech
Datarama — 118

Habitat
Home mobile — 122
Monique Eleb — 126
« Modulable »
Cédric Simonin, Des logements 100 % évolutifs — 128
Datarama — 130

04 BIEN-ÊTRE

Santé
Le temps de la médecine augmentée — 136
Mohamed Hajjam — 140
Surveillance sur ordonnance
Joël de Rosnay — 142
L'avènement d'un modèle préventif et participatif
Datarama — 144

Alimentation
Abdel Alaoui, Show devant ! — 148
À quel saint se vouer ? — 152
Olivier Lepiller — 156
La chasse au naturel
Charles Boes — 158
Au régime des IA
Datarama — 160

Boissons
En pleine effervescence — 164
Magali Caulman — 168
Penser global, boire local
H.Theoria — 170
Coup de jus sur les spiritueux
Datarama — 172

05 CULTURE

Jouets
Double jeu — 178
Aurélien Fouillet — 182
S'éduquer au numérique
Frédérique Tutt — 184
« Ça change, mais lentement »
Datarama — 186

Enseignement
Quand le digital fera école — 190
Alain Goudey — 194
La fin du one best way
Antoine Amiel, Vers un apprentissage plus agile — 198
Datarama — 198

Médias
La mutation de l'information — 202
Rémy Rieffel — 206
« Journalisme enrichi »
Mathieu du Poset, Trouver une communauté de lecteurs — 208
Datarama — 210

Art
Enki Bilal — 214
Et si Internet disparaissait d'un coup ?
Augmenter l'exposition — 220
Pierre-Yves Lochon — 224
Sortir le musée de ses murs
Jean Vergès, Le Neuilly de l'art — 226
Datarama — 228

Tourisme
Lost in transition — 232
Rodolphe Christin — 236
La crise du surtourisme
Aurélien Seux — 238
Trop avise
Datarama — 240

Lost in transition

Photographie — Benjamin Rousselle

LE FLÉAU DU SURTOURISME

Trop de tourisme tue le tourisme ! Crise de surfréquentation des sites touristiques, standardisation de ce qui devrait rester une aventure, impact environnemental élevé : l'industrie des vacances est en panne de sens. Quelles pistes pour se réinventer ?

Si partir ailleurs fait toujours rêver, la surfréquentation des sites devient problématique. Dans plusieurs grandes villes européennes, l'augmentation du nombre de visiteurs endommage les monuments historiques et empoisonne la vie des citadins. À tel point que la résistance s'organise. À Rome, les bus de touristes ne sont plus admis dans le centre historique depuis début 2019. À Venise – 25 millions de touristes annuels pour 55 000 habitants –, la mairie a voté, le 1er mai 2019, une taxe de 3 euros par journée passée sur place afin de financer le nettoyage de la ville. À Amsterdam, à Barcelone, à Reykjavik, c'est le même refrain. Il faut faire baisser le nombre de touristes. Idem au Pérou où l'accès au Machu Picchu va être limité à deux temples et une pyramide, afin de préserver ce joyau de l'architecture inca qui subit les assauts de 600 000 visiteurs tous les ans.

Mais ces désagréments ne sont que la partie émergée de l'iceberg. Le tourisme a en effet exporté partout dans le monde le mode de vie particulièrement polluant des sociétés industrialisées. Déchets plastique, destruction des écosystèmes,

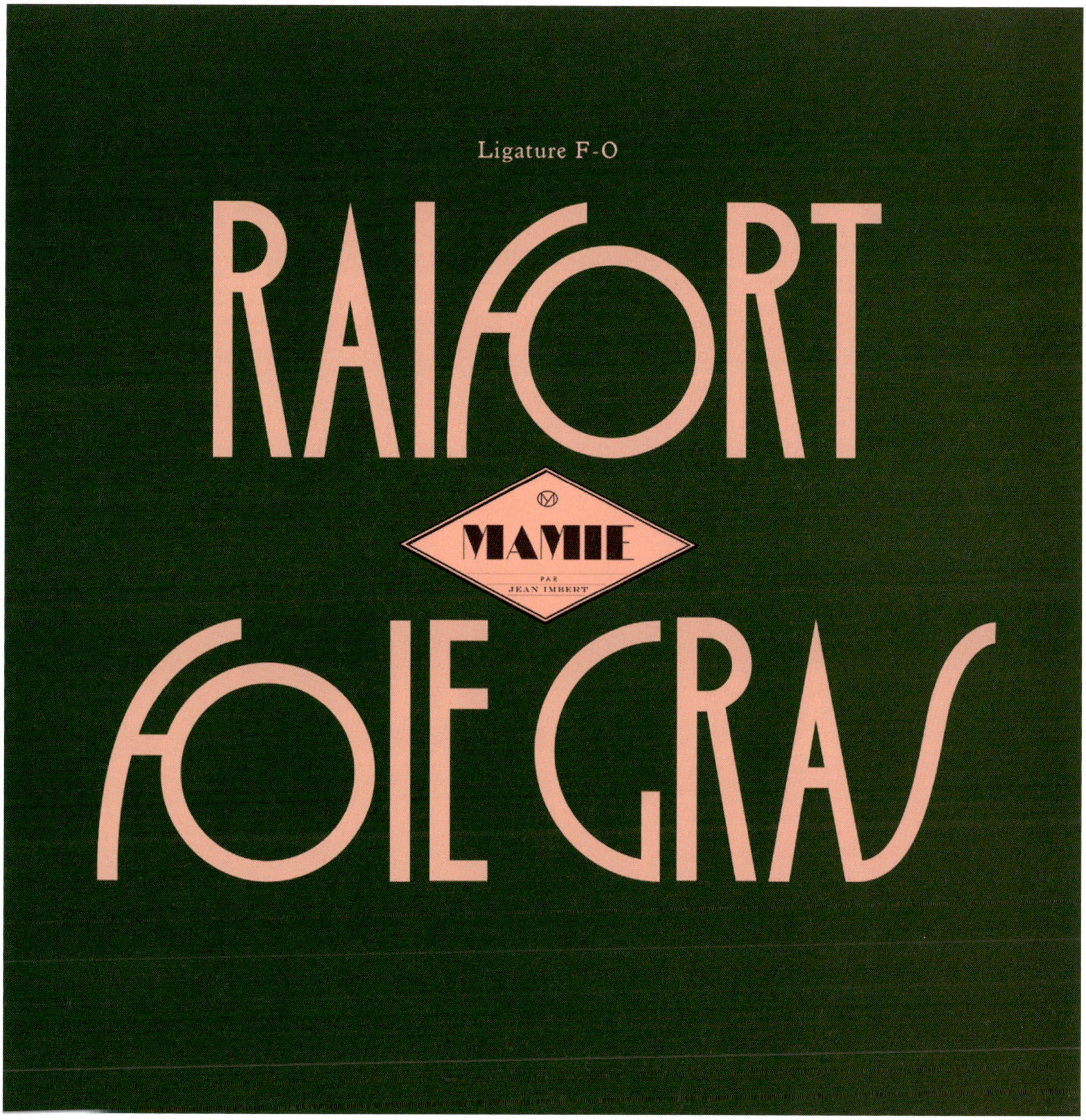
Ligature F-O
RAIFORT
MAMIE
PAR
JEAN IMBERT
FOIE GRAS

Secondary custom font
A
@mamie
MAMIE

BAR
MAMIE
Secondary custom font

MAMIE

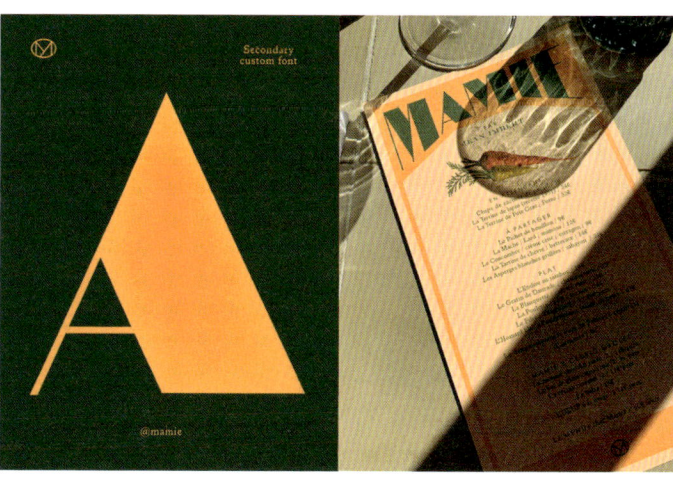

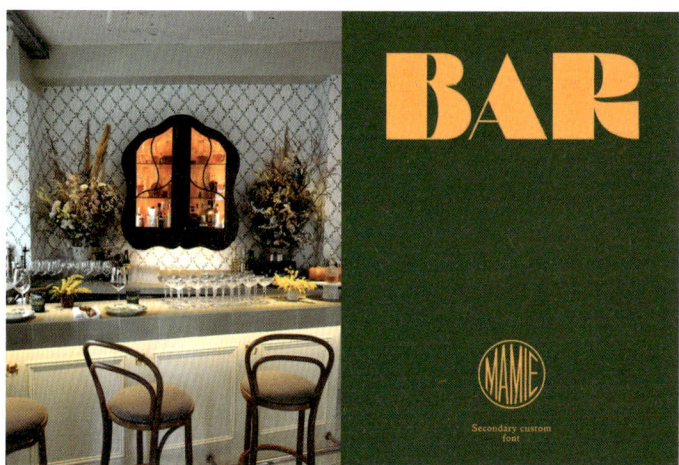

Dialogue with LEWIS McGUFFIE

Lewis McGuffie

A type designer from the UK. Majored in the MA Typeface Design (MATD), he graduated from the University of Reading in 2019. McGuffie won the Granshan Grand Prize for non-Latin scripts in 2019, and was a fina-list in the Morisawa Typeface Design Competition (Latin category). His typeface Tusker is the brand font for the England Rugby team.

Interviewer
Gakky Luk

SHORTCUTS IN DESIGN

HONG

gh Pylon

NG HAUL EXPEDITION

Tusker

GREEN BELT—PROFICIENCY IN TYPE DESIGN

CINDIE ②
/ A 126PT

Cindie

Q&A

You have customized typefaces for a number of brands. What is the key to designing suitable typefaces for brands?

So far, I have worked on fonts for lifestyle products—food, drink, music, sport, etc. These are not essential products—just fun stuff to buy, so the branding needs to look really attractive to the right audiences who are willing to spend money. Understanding the history of the brand, what the product is and where it is from are the key points. For example, when I made a typeface for a distillery called Lahhentagge, I visited the small island where the product is from. There were old rural churches in fields, small villages, forests and lots of Viking history there. The ingredients for the gin all came from that place too. So, I drew the typeface with a historical, runic, and organic feeling—just like a Viking carving the letters into stone!

You graduated with a master's degree in the major of Typeface Design of the University of Reading. How has this experience helped in your design?

Reading's MATD was brilliant. It was an opportunity to meet interesting people in the industry, learn a lot and see the huge archive they have there. The course has a strong focus on research and writing, which I really enjoyed. I wrote my dissertation on the history of and methods for designing bold weights in Latin. That was a challenge, but a lot of fun. The environment is perfect for growing and learning as a type designer. The course also requires doing non-Latin scripts, and with the professors and tutors available it is possible to learn any writing system on the MATD. I did Greek, Cyrillic and Hebrew (as well as Latin of course) in my final project. The Greek and Cyrillic I drew won the 2019 Granshan Grand Prize for non-Latin scripts, for which I was very grateful. Also last year I started drawing some Chinese characters with the help of a Chinese PhD student. This process was very difficult, but interesting to learn how that writing system works.

Do you have any preferences when you design typeface?

I haven't designed many italics, although I like them. I also really like incised serifs like Wolpe's Albertus, for example. I am trying to design an incised serif at the moment. But I don't really have a preference. I like anything that can provide a challenge to my workflow. While I am drawing, if I stumble over a certain letter and am forced to really think about it and do more research, then I enjoy that and I feel like I am learning. Or, if I am working on extended alphabets, I enjoy devising new useful kerning strings. I like devising methods, scripts and shortcuts for solving problems that occur with any new design. It is the problem-solving aspect that I enjoy most about typeface design. It's a visual art that through research, engages with time, place, aesthetics, and so on, but it is underpinned by a methodology of engineering and good practice.

Dialogue with TWOPOINTS.NET

TwoPoints.Net

Based in Hamburg, Berlin and Barcelona, the design studio was founded in 2007 with the aim of doing exceptional design work. TwoPoints.Net is a small company that thinks big. Not just in terms of international clients, but with their network as well. Clients include the Picasso Museum Barcelona, National University of Singapore, IBM, Volkswagen (DE) among others.

Interviewer
Gakky Luk

GREEN BELT — PROFICIENCY IN TYPE DESIGN

Changing the Design Methodology

ESPN Next

A typeface cannot be designed in one day. Most of the time, the ideas of designing a new typeface depend on designer's daily accumulation of inspiration. How do you accumulate such inspiration?

Actually designing a font can be done in a day if it does not have much details, but finding the right concept can take years. It requires a lot of knowledge, experiences and experiments to find a new idea. Technical skills do not amaze me anymore. This just takes time. But I am amazed when I see someone coming up with a new idea, considering the amount of type out there.

You have mentioned that "Visual outcome is the result of our research, concept and strategy." What research will you do before designing a new typeface?

We mainly design custom fonts for visual identities. Before we design them, we need to learn about our clients' product, message, market and target audience to be able to design a (visual) strategy and concept.

Since its establishment in 2007, has TwoPoints.Net ever changed its methodology of type design? What is the most difficult part and the most interesting part in the process of type design for you?

We are changing our methodology with almost every new project. Designing your process has a huge effect on the result. Right now we are experimenting with kinetic type design, which means that we design type in Cinema 4D. This gives us a whole lot of new possibilities to play with.

Dialogue with DANIEL McQUEEN

Daniel McQueen

McQueen is the founder of The Designers Foundry (hereinafter referred to as "TDF"). Since 2012, TDF has been making quality, accessible and interesting typeface. It's a hand-picked international team of type designers who strive to provide all designers with a quality supply of curated typefaces that is constantly evolving. TDF has licensed their typefaces to an array of customers, from students and studios all the way to major international clients such as Apple, Nike, Netflix, MTV, Virgin, Random House and GAP, to name just a few.

Interviewer
Gakky Luk

EXPAND THE DESIGN INDUSTRY

Tomato Grotesk

A Non-Reader for people who like to look at letters

Also known as Specimen

Morion Typeface
2019

P 00

Q&A

Founded in 2012, TDF has designed 58 font families. How do you continuously carry out such an amount of type design work while also guaranteeing the quality of the typefaces?

Our 58 (and growing) typefaces are designed by 36 individual designers from all around the world, most of the designers on our website only have 1-2 typefaces released. The typefaces range in design and development time, from anywhere between 6 months to 7 years, depending on the typeface. We've been open for 9 years, some of the typefaces we offer have been having updates and refinement for this whole time.

More and more people are paying attention to type design recently. Is this the same in New Zealand? How is type design valued in New Zealand?

Being a small industry in a small country, type design doesn't have much of an understanding or appreciation here by the general public, but I imagine this is something that's not exclusive to New Zealand. Generally, those that are aware of type design in New Zealand are as you would expect: graphic designers, etc. However the design industry is also small, so we rarely sell fonts to locals, but it is slowly growing with time. The locals that do license from us have a fair understanding of the value of using good typefaces and proudly support us.

As the technology is developing, there are more and more cutting-edge tools for designers. Facing with this change or challenge, what do you think font designers need to do?

In the face of changing technology, type designers need to ensure they're educated and understand the changing tools around them and if appropriate, put them to use for their advantage.

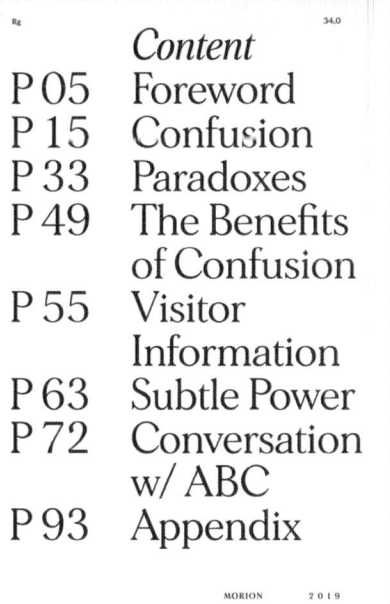

VINTAGE LETTERING EXPERIMENTS

AD, CD & D
Thom Niessink

DS
Thom Niessink

2020

36 Days of Type is a yearly open call inviting designers, illustrators and visual artists to share their views on the letters and numbers from the Latin alphabet.
    This year, the designer created a series that was inspired by letter shapes, effects and colors from the 1950s to the 1970s. All the designs were sketched on an iPad first using Procreate, then vectorized using Glyphs and Illustrator. The retro effects and final touches were applied in Photoshop.

053 GREEN BELT—PROFICIENCY IN TYPE DESIGN

MONDWEST & NEUEBIT TYPEFACES

AD
Mathieu Desjardins
(Pangram Pangram® Foundry)

CD
Steve Marchal (Datalaze)

D
Steve Marchal &
Pangram Pangram® Foundry

DS
Pangram Pangram® Foundry &
Datalaze

2016-2020

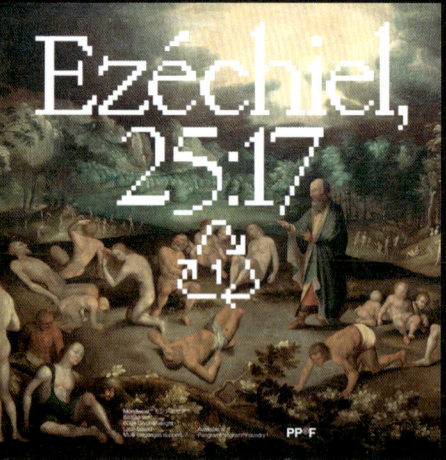

Designed to be users' next go-to pixel font, these bitmap fonts were inspired by the classic Grotesk and Serifs of the designers' era. With more than 600 characters, these were crafted for maximum legibility, versatility and pairing capacity.

NeueBit™ BoldCE 28 Opt 600 Gl. OTF-

NeueBit™ was born in the past
and did live its entire life in the future.
It is brought back to you today
by PangramPangram® Foundry.

NeueBit™ is a serif bitmap latin-based typeface
w/ multi-languages support, general punctuation,
japanese katakana's, extended latin, greek capital letters,
superscripts & subscripts, fractions, arrows, japanese
katakana's, and few symbols for you to play with.
This typeface comes with two weights: Regular & Bold,
and does contain 600 glyphs on each weight.

Designed (with love) by Steve Marchal
in collaboration with PP®F Montréal, CA.
All rights reserved @PP®F - 2020.

NeueBit™
is a free-to-try font!
→ pangrampangram.com

SNOT

AD, CD & D
Søren Steenstrup Højen

DS
Sunfried Studio

2016

BØRN
SPISER
SNOT

ABCDEFGHIJ
KLMNOPQRST
UVWXYZÆØÅ

The designer wanted to make a playful font, which children would enjoy. What came most strongly to his mind were three things. The first was cozy but slightly dusty memories of holidays in Poland where the designer remembered witnessing strange bombastic fonts. As a Scandinavian with a minimalistic tradition, these fonts were strange to the designer but also fascinating to look upon. Another memory that inspired him was the feeling of looking at green slime, and how it constantly changed shape. The final thing that perhaps inspired him the most were the strangely shaped figures which are known as gogo's.

057 GREEN BELT—PROFICIENCY IN TYPE DESIGN

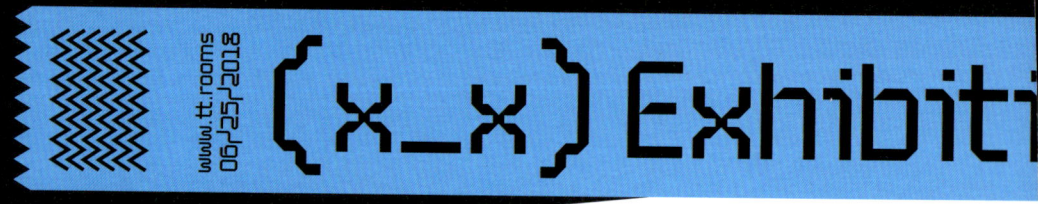

TECHTAPE FONT

CD & D
Nastia Piven

2018

Techtape Font is a typeface based on the idea of folding and cutting tape strips making lines, angles and new shapes. The designer was inspired by an ordinary black tape that was used a lot to stick sketches on the walls of design spaces while working on various projects. Techtape is masculine, geometric and structured. It has its rules and limitations, but at the same time it is still lively, bold and emotional.

ABCDEFGH
IJKLMNOPQ
RSTUVWXYZ
CC CG OO Œ TT
TW TY Th UB UD

æ cky œ ee ff fb fh fi fj fl
fr ft fy ffb ffh ffi ffj ffl ffr fft
ffy gg gi gy ggy ip it ky

1234567890

AD, CD & D
Casper Schutte

DS
Spook Design Co.

2020

DOPPELGANGER

Doppelganger is a free display serif typeface. It is a vintage-inspired font that is ideal for project where a delicate touch is needed. The project was created during the 5-month lockdown in South Africa, to cope with the stresses and frustrations that came with this difficult time. The designer was fascinated by the strange ligatures on vintage typefaces and wanted to pay homage to a bygone era while still creating a fun modern font.

TOCCO

CD
Gustavo Garcia

D
Thiago Bellotti

DS
Papanapa

2020

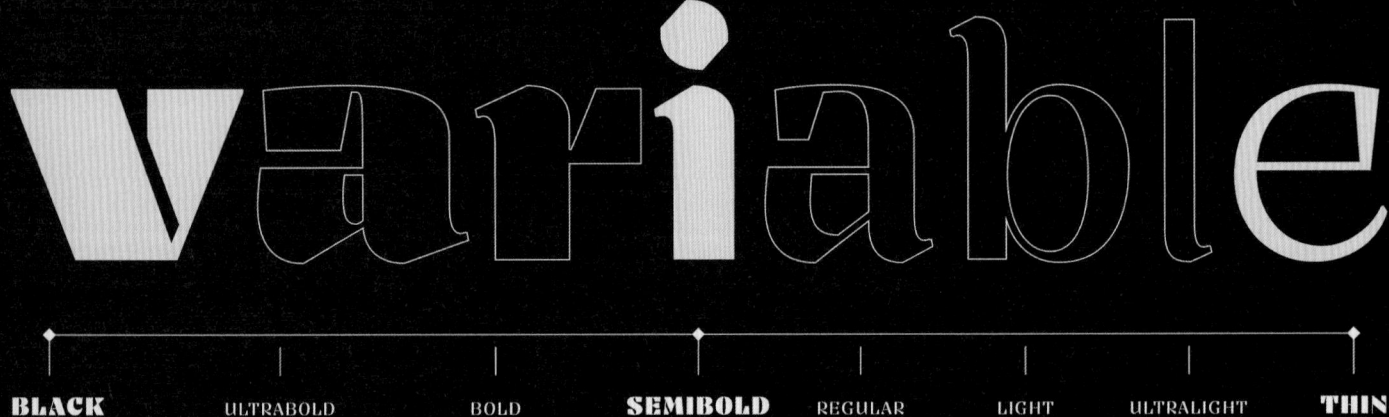

Tocco is a high contrast variable font available in eight weights. Inspired by leftover chunks of wood found in a workshop, its angular curves and sharp serifs established a bold and elegant visual personality when used on headlines and solid displays. Tocco provides standard ligatures and extends multilingual support to Basic Latin and Western European.

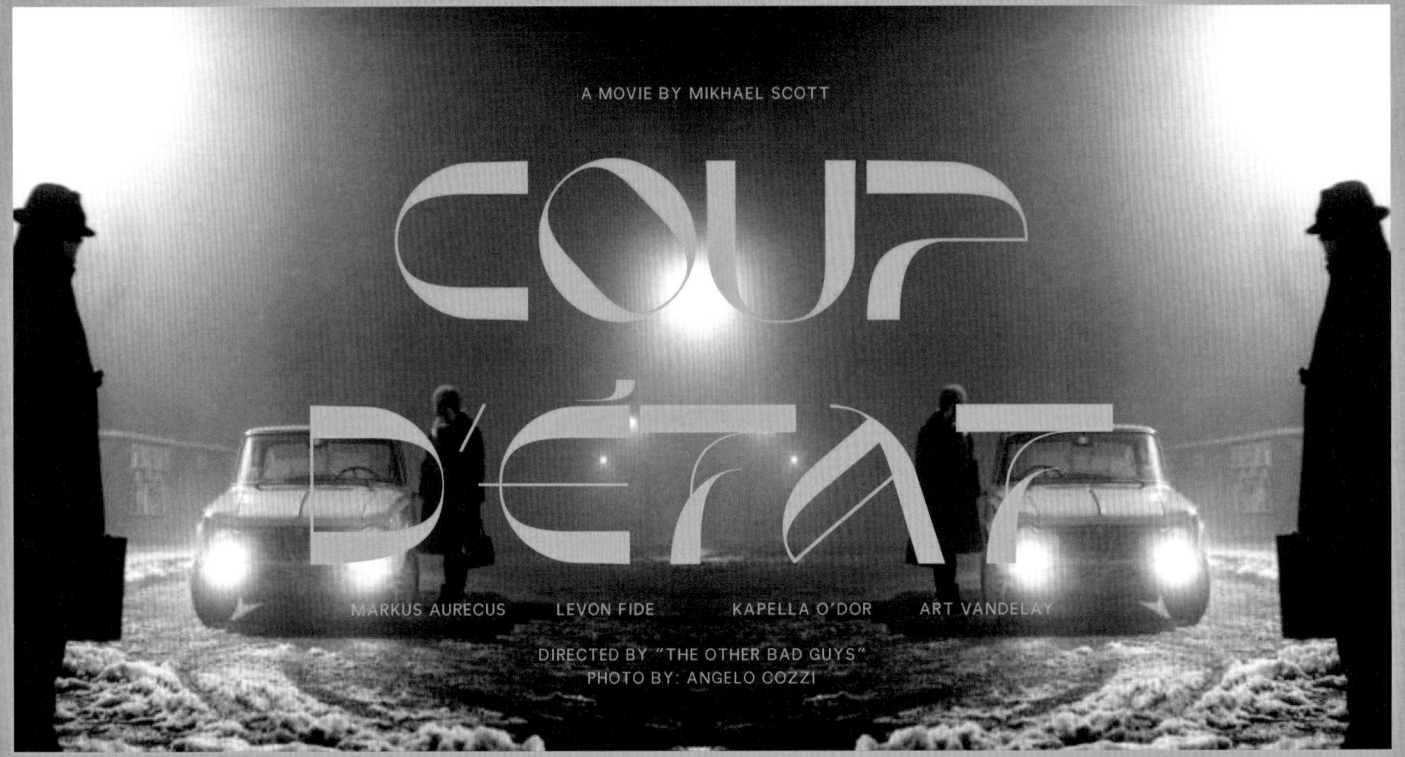

E_P Ligature

E_R Ligature

E_S Ligature

E_X Ligature

E_S_R Ligature

J_J Ligature

L_J Ligature

F_R Ligature

O_O Ligature

L_L Ligature

S_R Ligature

T_T Ligature

ROCHELLE
ROCHELLE

AYYA'DEN BERI

FUTURISTIK URETMLER

4517 WASHINGTON AVE.

MANCHESTER, KENTUCKY

39495

COSTES GRACILIS

AD, CD & D
Murathan Biliktü

DS
Cognoscenti Studio

2020

The project was inspired by the last sunset and the summer breeze on the Mediterranean coast. Gracilis is the sequel to the first font made by the designer: Costes. The designer wanted to make a more slender and version with heavy contrast. The contrast between the rounded body of the type and the sharpness in the edges makes the designer think of it as if it was made by an extraterrestrial being.

FUNKY EXPERIMENTATION ALPHABET

Nubia Navarro Aka Nubikini

D

2020

36 Days of Type is an awesome and very popular project where designers, artists and other creatives design one letter a day for one month. The designer has always liked funky and retro shapes, so this time the designer tried something with that style. And the designer drew inspiration from mid-century shapes and tried to merge them with plain Bauhaus characteristic colors.

SHRIFTOVIK font foundry presents

↓ ↓ ↓ ↓ ↓ ↓ ↓ ↓ ↓ ↓ ↓ ↓

new handwritten typeface

ABCDEFGHIJKLMNOPQRSTUVWXYZÀÁÂÃÄĂÅ
ĄÆÐĆĈĊČĒĔĖĘĚÊËĘĜĞĠĢĤĦÌÍÎĨĪĬĮĶĹĽ
ŁÑŃŅŊÒÓŎŌÔÖØǾŒŘŔŖŚŠŜŞŢŦŤÙÚŨŬŮŪ
ÜŰŲŴẂŴẀÝŶŹŻŽÞabcdefghijklmnopqrstuvwxyzàá
âãäåąæçćĉċčďđēĕėęěêëĝğġģĥħìíîĩīĭįķĺľłñń
ņŋòóŏōôöøǿœŕŗśšŝşţŧť'úũūŭůųŵẃŵẁýŷźżžþß

0123456789 ¹ ⁰ ² ³ ¼ ½ ¾ . , : ; … « » " " ` ,, " ' ! ? ¿ ¡ † ‡ # & §
@ % ‰ < > - – — _ / \ ¦ | ( ) { } [ ] № ∆ ◊ • + − * = ≠ × ≤ ≥ ± ∞ ¬
≈ ~ ∆ √ ∫ ƒ ¤ Σ ∕ ≡ ← ↑ → ↓ ↔ ∂ ℓ ∂ ∏ ¶ ° ∇
ﬀ ﬁ ﬂ ﬃ ﬄ ℗ ® © ™
$ ¢ € £ ₽ ₣ ₺ ¥

AD, CD & D
Tikhon Reztcov

DS
SHRIFTOVIK font foundry

2020

SK MORALIST

SK Moralist is an authentic handwritten font. It was inspired by the style of ink-writing techniques. The font's smooth and rounded shapes give it an unusual and unique look. This font is multilingual and supports all Latin and Cyrillic languages, including an extended Latin alphabet. It also supports the Greek alphabet. Therefore, the font is suitable for use in almost every country or region.

D
Nastya Novikova
2020

TYPOGRAPHY EXPERIMENTS CHALLENGE

This is a design to participate the global project—36 Days of Type.
   Each letter designed by a participating designer should be unique, and the most important thing was to try something new. The hope is to encourage designers to find fresh ideas, improve their skills, push forward and never give up! All the letters look like scattered colored stickers, with each one representing a new day and a new idea behind it.

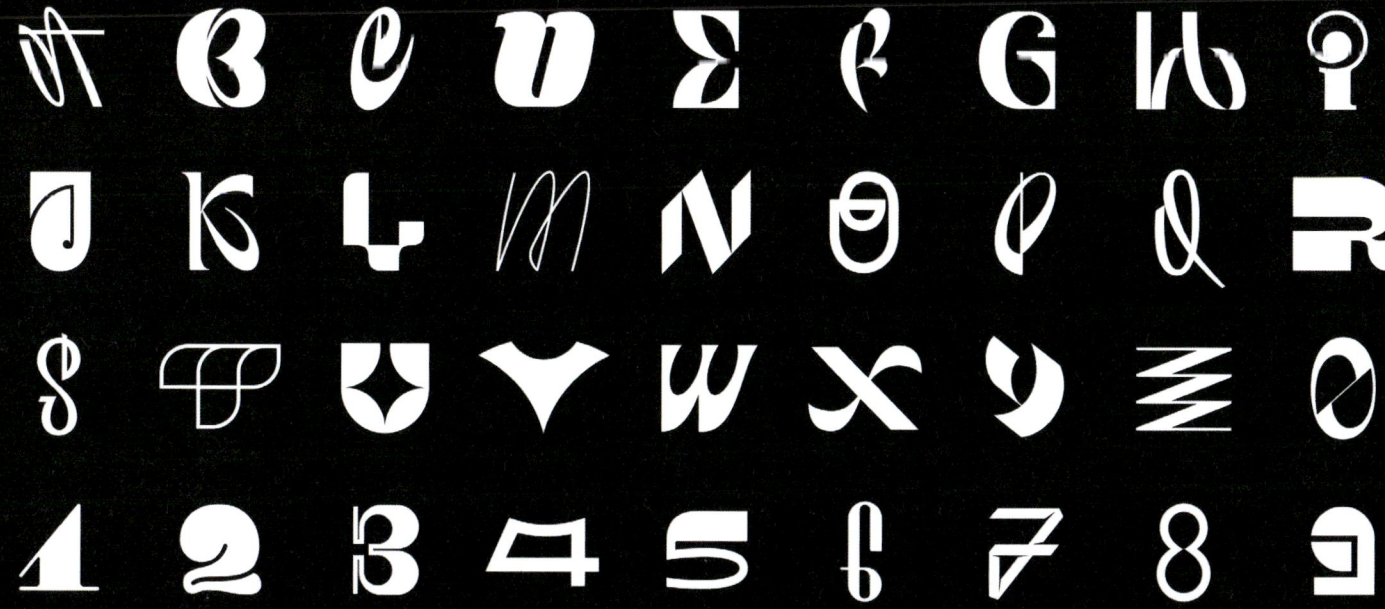

AÁĂÂÄÀĀĄÅÃÆBCĆ
ČÇĊDĐĎÐEÉĚÊËĖÈĒĘẼ
FGĞǦĢĠHĦIÍĬÎÏİÌĪĮĨJKĶ
LĹĽĻŁMNŃŇŅŊÑOÓÔÖ
ÒŐŎŌØÕŒPÞQRŔŘŖSŚŠ
ŞȘẞTŦŤŢṬUÚÛÜÙŬŰŪŲŮ
VWẂŴẄẀXYÝŶŸỲZŹŽŻ
?¿!..,;[](){}-–—_""«»#%"*§¶@•
††∂∏∑√∫™∞©®£¢α¥€μ◊≈≤≥
1234567890 1234567890

Solar
Version 2018
Typeface

Solar
Version 2020
Typeface

D & P
Gwennina Moigne

2018-2019

SOLAR TYPEFACE

Solar is a revival of the typeface Romain du Roi, a font commissioned by King Louis XIV of France in 1692. In February 2019, the designer presented this project at the Type Directors Club during a Type Thursday event and gained numerous helpful feedback. Then, in March 2020, the designer decided to launch this new version of Solar Typeface.

ALPHABET

AD, CD & D
Carmen Nacher Rodriguez

2020

This project is an alphabet design challenge launched by the Instagram Account @36daysoftype. The emphasis of this project was on the designer creating an alphabet where all the letters would keep to the same line or style, while maintaining sufficient characterization to stand up alone as single designs. The designer wanted to create playful typefaces through exaggerating the parts of each letter in order to almost personify them, all the while maintaining the structural rigor of traditional weights in its structure so all letters would still be instantly recognizable.

GREEN BELT — PROFICIENCY IN TYPE DESIGN

BARBAROS FONT FAMILY

D
Mahmoud Abdelghany

DS
Abdelghanyart Design Studio

2020

* DISPLAY ART DECO FONT WITH 8 STYLES *

BARBAROS

بربروس

* خط طباعي للعناوين بثمانية أوزان *

Barbaros is a condensed Art Deco display sans font with 8 styles, 800 glyphs, 100 ligatures, 30 languages and many Opentype features. What makes Barbaros font family unique is the "block" weight, which has all letters blocked without "inner spaces", something that makes it very powerful for headlines and posters particularly. It is perfect for use in poster design, magazine, book cover, logotype, headline, newspaper, and publication.

لما
موشن

حضارة مصر الفرعونية

LA CASA DE PAPEL
THE WALKING DEAD

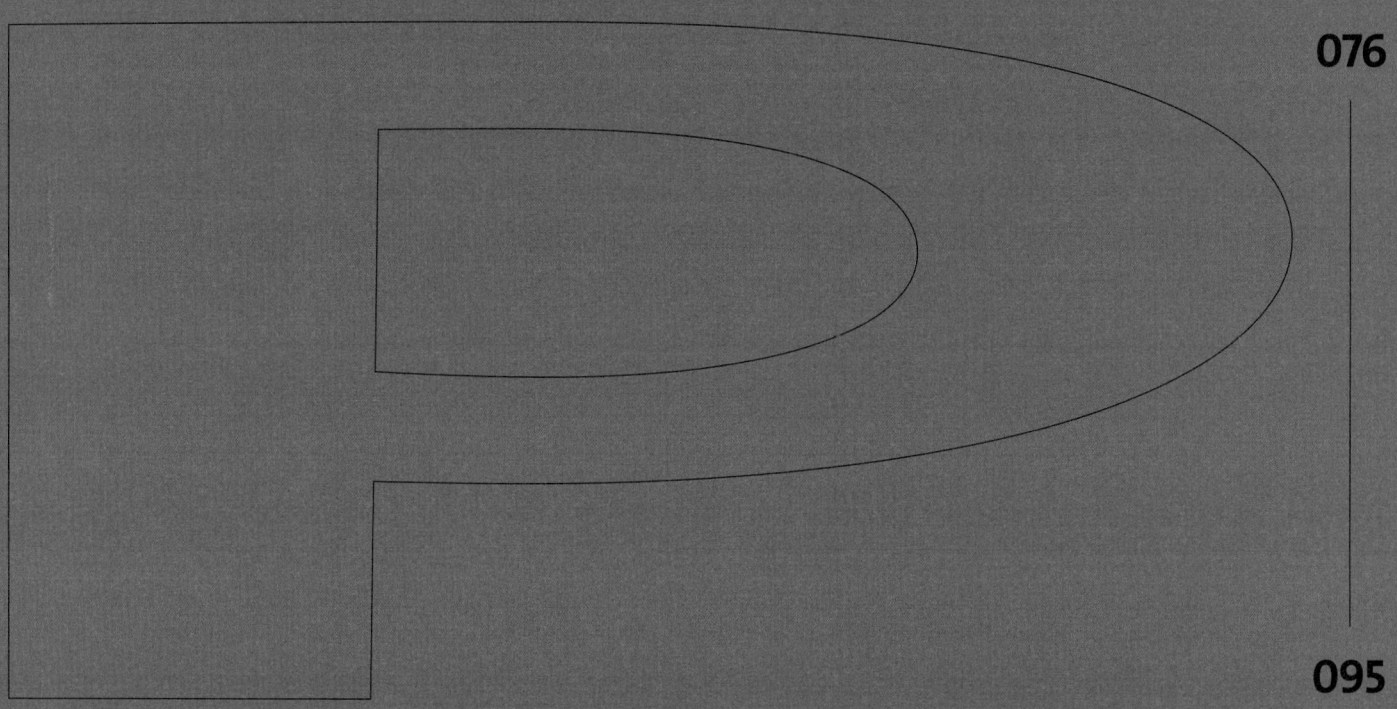

Type designers need to combine their expertise in their native language system and design knowledge when creating a multilingual typeface. In addition, they need to also take into account the influences of the cultural background of other languages, in order to present the features of each language in a unified and integrated way through their designed typefaces. Similarly, when judokas are in the process of studying for their blue belt, they should focus not only on themselves but also on the possible reactions of their opponents in the contest when using various techniques. In this case, it involves the influences of the second subject in the contest.

ARTISTIC AND LIBERAL TRANSLATION

Editor
Gakky Luk

to a new world. Before one can acquire a new language, a faithful, expressive reader with the profound culture behind the language. With such a translation, all the implied emotion inherent in Soseki Natsume's poetic line: "The moon is beautiful, leisurely scene or the bleakness in the five-character quatrains. Or one can feel the beauty through the strict structure of Shakespeare's sonnets. Such a conception of translation need not only field of literature, it also has connotations that have gradually emerged in other fields.

increasing prominence of multinational enterprises in the Chinese market and the development of China's tionals in recent years, more and more companies focus on the "visual translation" of their logos in order to gap and integrate their own unique brand culture into the target market. Visual translation requires the logo into one in the target language and retain the same characteristics and temperament ual translation is a challenging task for designers, because it requires a solid foundation uct is introduced to a different region or country, it is easy to make mistakes within to cultural barriers. An awareness of transcultural design ensures that the monstrable understanding of, and respect for each culture. For example, Cocaer, an elegant typeface, as the typeface of its iconic logo. In order to corresponhen, the designer of the Chinese logo, replaced the beginning and ending stroIn addition, he inclined the logo to a certain angle, so as to strengthen the logos in terms of style and feature, creating an individualized brand imagesed designer TienMin Liao launched a project named Bilingual Lettering, wresponding logotype styles between Chinese and English scripts through 50

Transcultural design not only involves logoign. Unlike experimental projects like Bilingual Lettering, type design is a syshe shape of characters, but it is the systematic thinking and research behinbecause it is closely related to culture, history, language, and a variety of designer, mentioned in the interview, "The relationship between language, cannot be discussed separately." Lisa Huang is a type designer who took part in the Google's Noto fonts. Similarly, the German designer Roman Wilhelm has designed Laowai Sunet Face from his distinctive perspective as a "cultural outsider". Such designers probe deeply into locastory, put forward their unique ideas based on their understanding and respect for the local culture, thus achievintegration between traditional culture and modern culture.

Dialogue with TIENMIN LIAO

TienMin Liao

Liao is an independent designer and typographer specializing in logotype development, typeface design and multi-script typography (Latin/Chinese/Japanese). Liao's works have been recognized by the Type Directors Club, Tokyo TDC and Morisawa Type Design Competition.

Interviewers
Nicole Lo & Gakky Luk

Reverse the Rules

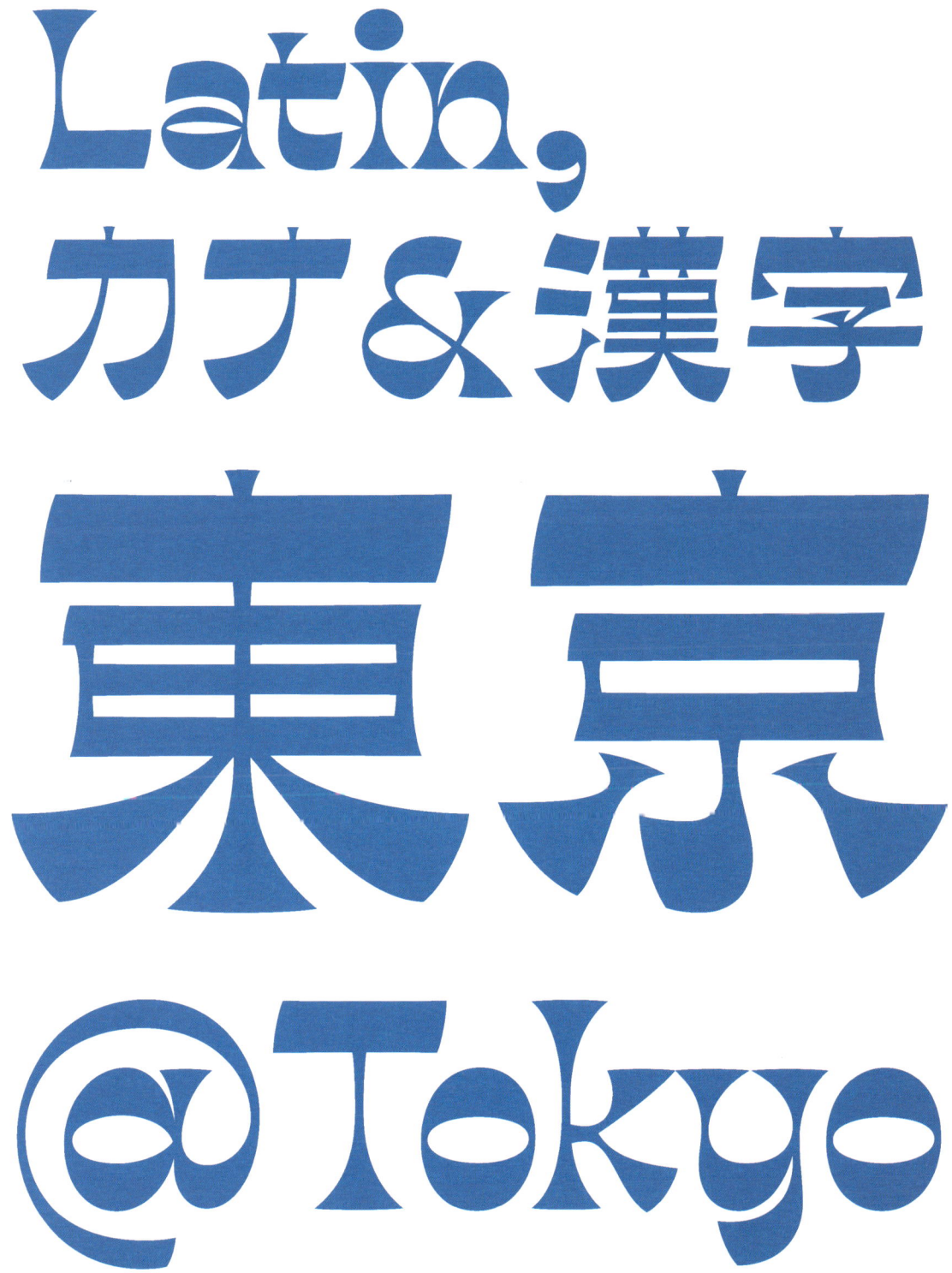

Ribaasu

チケット SOLD OUT

かな 漢字

ぷろ

TokyoDome 東京ドーム

ね

Google Home
は Spotify に
対応しています

&

麗しい

アマゾンエコー
で音楽を聴く

@ 48.3%

OSXユーザー 選

む

Ribaasu

Ribaasu

You launched the Bilingual Lettering project in 2016. How did you harmoniously combine simple Latin scripts with complex square characters to express the same characteristic and temperament?

Bilingual Lettering project is a series of Latin-Kanji pairing studies for use in bilingual lettering and logotype. Since these two writing systems are traditionally written with different tools, and the character structures are also very different, in order to inject the same personality into these two scripts, sometimes flexibility is necessary. Every single pair bilingual lettering is a custom result, so there isn't only one solution. There are a few approaches: 1. Pairing with the existing type genre based on their history. 2. Adding the features from the other script as decorative elements or drawing both scripts with the same tool. 3. Treat the type as a graphic. One approach may be better than the other under different circumstances. It depends on your needs.

You have designed logotypes for brands. What rules do you follow in the adaptation of logotypes?

There are two kinds of bi-scriptual logotype: 1. The two scripts are equally important. 2. One of them plays the main role and the other works as a supported role. For the first kind of bi-scriptual logotype, the most important criteria for designing a bilingual lettering is expressing the "same personality" in both scripts, under the premise of designing with legibility and basic type knowledge, rather than limiting to sharing a "similar appearance". For the second one, we can choose a less expressive typeface for the supported script.

You have designed a reverse-contrast typeface named Ribaasu, which can be used in Chinese characters, Japanese Kana and Latin scripts. Can you tell us about this typeface?

In a reverse-contrast typeface, the normal weight distribution is reversed. The result is that the weight becomes concentrated along the cap-height, x-height, and baseline, creating a strong horizontal visual connection.

Unlike the Latin alphabet, the weight distribution in Kanji and Kana is much more complex, and the weight is not just on the verticals. Many strokes are diagonal or curved, so the weight distribution varies on different strokes. Simply reversing the weight distribution may not create the same visual result as in the Latin one. Instead of reversing the weight literally, my approach is to create a typeface that captures the visual essence of the Latin reverse-contrast. That essence is the quirky personality and strong horizontal connection; thus, both can work together in a visually compatible way.

In addition to the rules above, I also integrated Clerical script (Li-shu/Reishotai) into the Kanji structure and the weight distribution in Ribbasu.

You are good at customizing logotypes and localizing Chinese characters. What factors should be considered in the localization of a typeface? Is there a standard?

A successful logotype localization should have the same or similar personality as the original one. In order to achieve this goal, we should not only focus on making the logotype visually consistent, but also need to understand the visual history and typography history behind the culture. Even within the Chinese speaking world, each area has different typographic culture. For instance, a certain typeface style might remind people of a historical event in one area, but might not work the same in the other place.

Do you think variable fonts will replace font-weight products?

I don't think it would completely replace the current font product right now. We have to see how it goes. Apple published their variable fonts 2 years ago, this could influence the industry a lot. Graphic designers would be one of the first groups that widely accept variable fonts. However, offering non-designers infinite choices may not be a great idea since they are not familiar with typesetting.

Some of my type design friends have fully embraced variable fonts. They are seeking new opportunities and potential in creating more interesting typefaces that haven't been done before. On the other side, some of them think variable font is not perfect and think that all the weights need to be manually checked and tested.

You've said that "Flexibility is important when designing a bilingual lettering." Did you encounter any problems during the process of combining the Chinese and Western fonts? How did you resolve these issues?

Usually the challenge comes from translating both the letterforms and visual element at the same time, especially when Latin one has been completed, which means there's no way to edit the Latin one. For instance, I was asked to translate a title of a video game with a "fire symbol" embedded in the wordmark last year. It's easy to have a symbol embedded in between the Latin letterforms, but it became very challenging for Hanzi due to the complexity of the Chinese characters. It is hard to make the symbol and the Hanzi look as a whole. I ended up needing to break the Hanzi a little bit to fit the symbol into it.

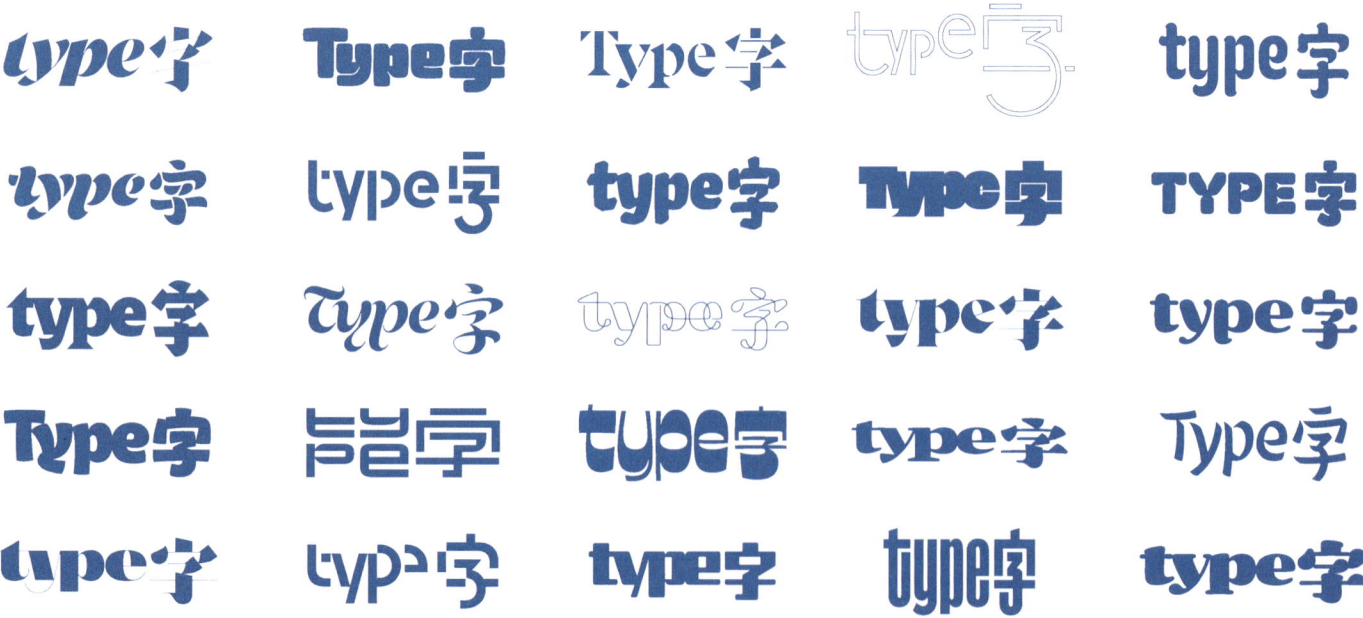

Bilingual Lettering

BLUE BELT—ADVANCED COMPREHENSION AND SKILLS

San Francisco **New York**
okyo London *Philadelphi*
São Paulo **Amsterdam** H
Milano Ürümqi **Munich**
Reykjavík **Taipei** Barcelor
hicago *Beijing* Mexico C
Paris Los Angeles **Sydney**
Osaka Berlin *Bangkok* Pa
e Janeiro **Montreal** *Rom*
ssen–Düsseldorf **Istanbu**

Min Sans

Dialogue with ROMAN WILHELM

Roman Wilhelm

A German-based communication designer and researcher. He studied visual communication at Burg Giebichenstein University of Art and Design Halle in Germany, and received a master's degree in type design at the Academy of Visual Arts Leipzig. Wilhelm is a fluent Chinese speaker, and focuses on transcultural mediation, bilingual typography and type design. Typefaces designed by Wilhelm include Laowai Sung and Hong Kong Street Face. And his work has been exhibited in many places, such as Hamburg, Berlin, Seoul, Tokyo, Beijing, Hong Kong, etc.

Interviewer
Gakky Luk

BLUE BELT—ADVANCED COMPREHENSION AND SKILLS

Vision of "Laowai"

AR
Laowai
Sung

Hamburg 汉堡 12pt
Hamburg 汉堡 16pt
Hamburg 汉堡 20pt
Hamburg 汉堡 24pt
Hamburg 汉堡 28pt
Hamburg 汉堡 36pt

Laowai Sung

gong　gaai　haak

「港街黑」

HONG KONG STREET FACE

香港：你好　홍콩: 안녕하세요

ホンコン: 今日は　Hello Hong Kong

سلام عليكم يا هونغ كونغ

九龍：早晨　주룽: 안녕히 주무셨어요

カオルン: 御早う　Good

morning Kowloon　صباح الخير يا كولون

Hong Kong Street Face

Compared to the Latin script, the structure of Chinese characters is more complex. As a German designer, how did you cross the boundary from a phonetic to an ideographic script during the design process?

At the time I started thinking about becoming a type designer in the future, I already spoke some Chinese and my editorial design jobs were almost exclusively linked to China—I designed multilingual printed or online matter for companies as well as academic exchange programs. In Germany, my clients wanted to know why I was more suitable for these jobs than other people. That is why I frequently had to explain basic questions about the differences between Latin and Chinese typography before a job even started, which made me aware of my potential of designing type on a multi-script level in the first place. In the early 2000s, finding books on Chinese typography was not as easy as it is today, especially for a "laowai" (meaning "foreigner") like me. So I celebrated every little dust-covered booklet I could find on 美術字 (meaning "artistic calligraphy") in the bookstores of Shanghai, until finally after ten years, I had accumulated a basic understanding. My first font ever published was indeed a Latin-Chinese multi-script, unlike most designers who typically start with just one script, and try to deal with the difficulty of adapting to other scripts afterwards.

You once said that your dream is to design a Latin typeface suitable for Chinese Song typefaces. What are the characteristics that this typeface should have?

It should feature everything a Latin-Chinese font needs: full-width forms, half-width, third-width, quarter-width, annotation forms for Pinyin, and all those special characters such as the "m^2" glyph that OpenType may have, italics as well. In terms of design, the vertical metrics should be optimized to fit in an em box without letting the baseline stray too far from the ideal position. The question of whether the x-height should be high or not so high is left to be decided by the designer, depending on the context. My own approach was to make a multi-weight proportional typeface, but keeping the glyph width unchanged, no matter if light or bold—I call it "omnispace". If you change the weights of Chinese fonts, the lines don't change, unlike most Latin typefaces, which is why I think that this is important. There is no need for deliberate stylistic adaptations to fit the Song typeface aesthetics, but elements such as droplets, dots, triangles or hooks could visually link to each other. But as with all good couples, these mutual details work as long as they seem natural, instead of appearing too deliberate.

You taught calligraphy at Burg Giebichenstein University of Art and Design in Halle, Germany. Your Laowai Sung also has a handwriting style. What do you think about the impact of handwriting and calligraphy on type design?

Handwriting naturally exerts many parameters on the visual fabric of a typeface that would be difficult to emulate digitally. This leads to random differences in the dimensions of single letters, the shape of stroke outlines, ink blurbs, stylistic inconsistencies after coffee break, etc. Writing by hand automatically envelops the letter skeletons with a texture some may find artistic or aesthetic, but in a way these envelopes (to use a term from the field of electronic music) can help hold scripts as different as Latin and Chinese together in a dense web of visual parameters. Laowai Sung is a perfect example of this, as I actually did not dare to design a Chinese typeface—it was the envelope of an original outline drawing by hand which provided, scanned and digitally prepared, provided a mutual texture effectively holding the scripts together. A musician friend of mine said he was able to sing in dialect things which he would be embarrassed to sing in high German. In a way, handwriting can add this visual dialect twist to a typeface—with no one taking it too seriously, and you can actually dare more. I am convinced this is one of the core values of calligraphy classes here and today.

You designed Laowai Sung and Hong Kong Street Face from the special perspective of a foreigner. How did you balance the "sense of laowai" and the localization of your work? Did you encounter some difficulties during the design process?

"Laowai" as a term is a place holder to me—it came to me and seeped into me when I first came to China. The word seemed to follow me, although I did not know what it meant. Who am I? Roman? Xiǎodì? Siu2dai6? Laowai? Deep inside I know I can never be a master of anything, and my work can never fully satisfy me, for it could always be better. I hate to discover overlooked mistakes in the final proof of a design project I worked on. Concept and result always differ. I never had the feeling of having achieved anything near to perfection. Thus, not only as a person foreign to China, but also where I should be "at home with", I have a feeling of "mama huhu" (meaning "fair to middling") that has been predominant through my career. And now I am designing Chinese typefaces! There is no other choice for me but to turn the sense of imperfection into creative energy, and this is my art, my quest, and it is what I am best at probably.

It often happens that there is a collision with your own original knowledge system during the design process. How do you deal with this situation?

No matter if it is a simple job for a client or a complex and altruistic art project, the discrepancy between my personal view about what it actually is that I am doing and what others see in it can be huge. Say, I am fully convinced that I am creating a gender-neutral figure for an infographic, and my colleagues reply, "The figure looks very male, could you neutralize their gender a bit?" Then I suddenly become aware of the fact that they are totally right. The more I fear misconception, the more I appreciate my colleagues' help in making me see, literally, what I didn't see before. Now, scale this discrepancy up to a Chinese font. I am glad to have started my practice with an artistic project rather than with a job for a client, which would have been suicidal in the first place. Nonetheless, over the years I was working on Laowai Sung or Hong Kong Street Face, the perspectives offered by others of what these fonts actually represent, came drizzling in, slowly changing (improving) my sense of what I was actually doing. So much of our work is intuition. The ability to exploit fully your intuition but also to let external views on what you do positively influence your work is what we all need to learn in our everyday practice. My side work as a songwriter taught me it doesn't matter what you do as long as it is coherent and consolidated in its parts. If you work with several writing systems, it's implied that coherence can only be achieved by a system of visual bits and pieces from all of the systems, it will never fully inhabit just one of the boxes.

You once mentioned in an interview that "type designers tell stories". How do you think to tell a good story through type design?

Storytelling might have been overstretched as a term. However, there is a discussion about the authorship of designers going on in recent discourse. I would personally go as far as to say designers are never just neutral beings performing what others have developed, but much more they are contributing to the visual twist of narratives by providing elements, and intrinsically contributing to the distinct perception of a story. In reverse, I know well that people not in touch with design can develop a deep understanding of images, of the look-and-feel or symbolism of color, which is what I note every day when I work with scientists. Type design offers the choice of adding a different visual twist to a story—as long as the fonts are there, there is choice. By actively designing type, this twist can be individualized and can be even more precise. But that only works if you manage to get the balance right between what you think it is, and what others think it is.

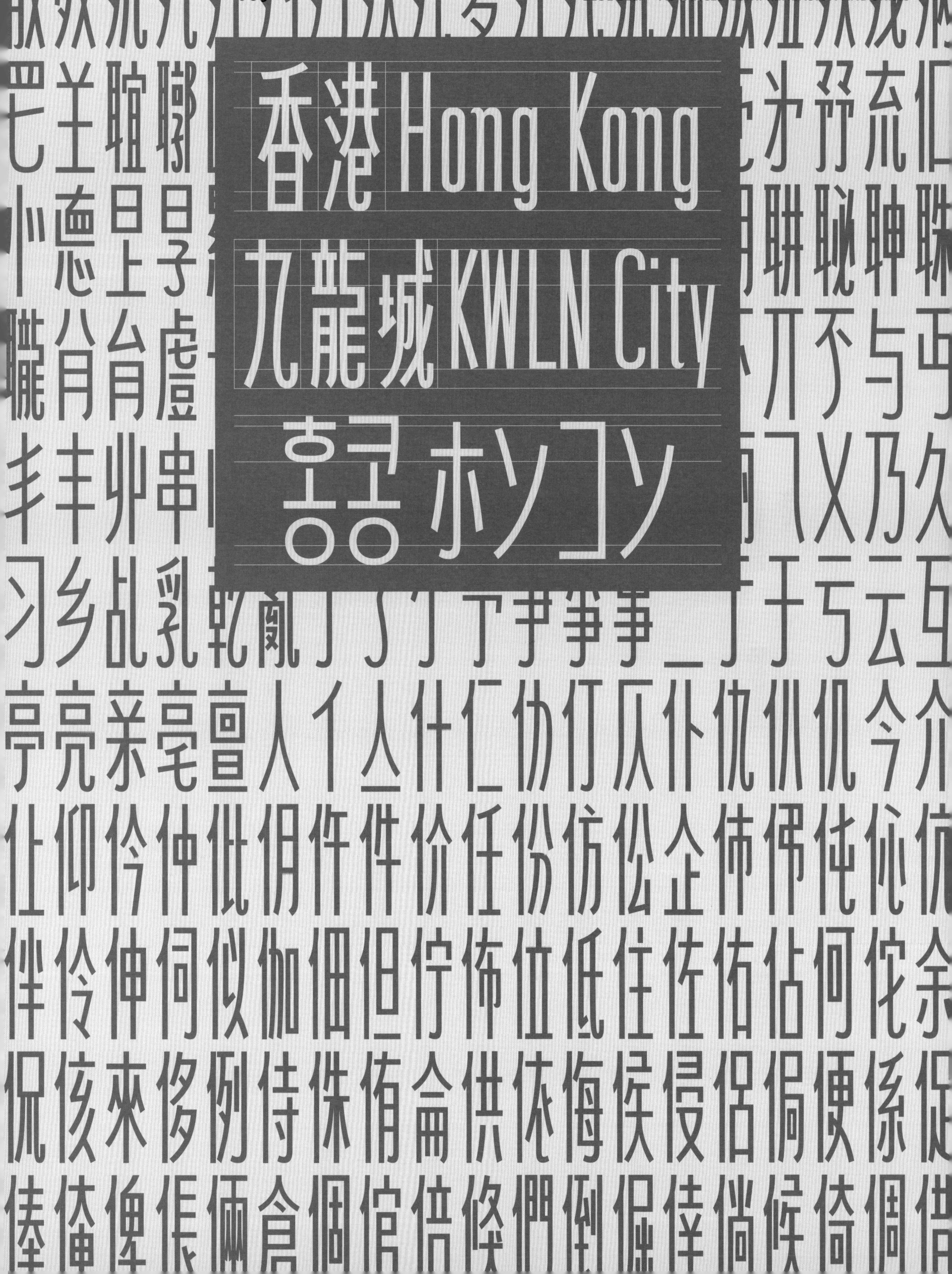

香港 Hong Kong
九龍城 KWLN City
홍콩 ホソコソ

Dialogue with LISA HUANG

Lisa Huang

An ethnic Chinese type designer and graphic designer who grew up in France. She studied graphic design in Paris, and in 2015, participated in the Type@Cooper program in New York to further her study in type design and typography. In 2018, Huang graduated with a master's degree in Type and Media from the Royal Academy of Art in the Hague. Huang is the type designer of Nüshu script for the Google Noto fonts.

Interviewer
Gakky Luk

BLUE BELT—ADVANCED COMPREHENSION AND SKILLS

Consistency between Design and Culture?

汉字

Hello
Latin

Noto Sans Nüshu

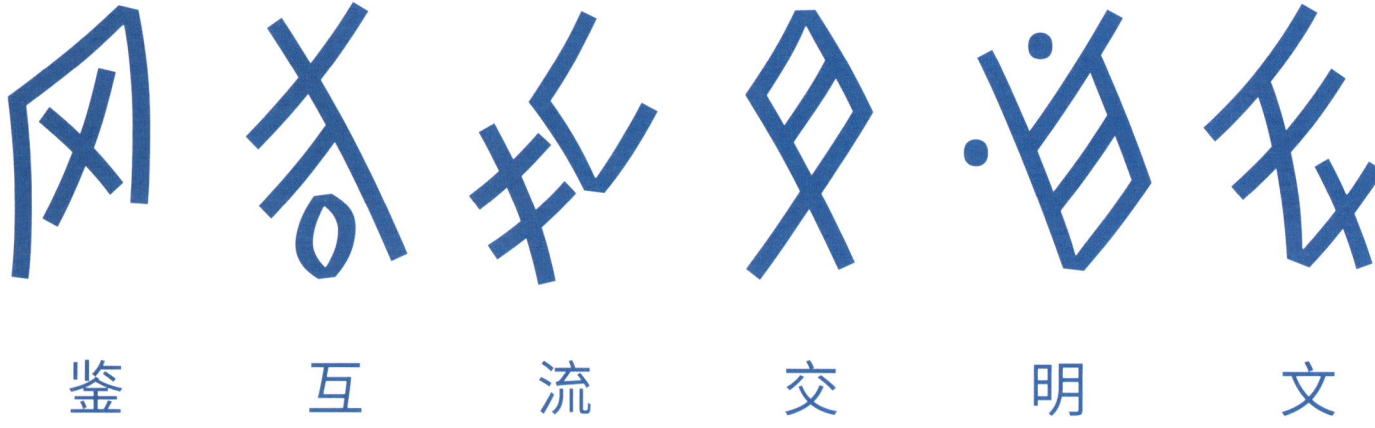

鉴　　　互　　　流　　　交　　　明　　　文

Noto Sans Nüshu

People often assume that understanding different languages allows designer to fully work in accordance with the cultures involved when designer carries out transcultural work. Do you think that it is necessary to acquire a language when designing a typeface?

Type design is the process of designing the visual appearance of a language. When designers understand the language they are designing, they can design shapes and details with an awareness of what they are doing—from the start to the end of the process—which is extremely important, especially for a typeface intended for usage with long texts.

But with display typefaces, even if the designer can't speak or write the language or script, they can still produce worthwhile designs using their creativity and experimentation. The safest approach, when in doubt, would be to check with a designer who is a daily user of that language.

I am not a user of Nüshu, so I would ask users of Nüshu to confirm the details of my work. In addition, I would also refer to relevant books or the shapes and proportions of calligraphy.

Nüshu script is most frequently seen as calligraphy, and there are all sorts of subtle differences. How did you deal with these details when designing Nüshu into a digital font?

Since there weren't any typefaces already designed when I started this project, I had to sort out everything that could be useful from a type design perspective and the details that could be considered as the script's "standards", to match with the design of Noto Sans in Latin and Chinese characters. I had to make this happen by sorting out samples from books, calligraphy and all sorts of documents, place them side by side for comparison, and the details that occured most frequently could be considered as "standard".

As a French-Chinese type designer, why are you interested in Nüshu script? Would you have any concerns that the typeface you designed may not be accepted by the local culture?

I chose to be a type designer because this creative field includes many aspects that are particularly interesting: art, crafts, history, technology, and culture, just to name a few. The reason why I design Latin and Chinese typefaces is that the scripts are the ones I use every day. Although I can't read nor write Nüshu, its feminine characteristics, shapes and history caught my curiosity.

In terms of making something that will be consistent with Nüshu culture, this was exactly what I was concerned about the most when designing such an unfamiliar script. This is why I put a lot of focus on comparing samples, avoiding personal preferences of certain details and rather respecting what I was seeing. Even with all that, I still had the shapes and results "validated" by actual Nüshu users. The whole challenge of this project was to design this script to make it consistent with two main criteria: typeface design "requirements" and Noto Sans design.

When designing Nüshu typeface, you researched a lot of related materials and conducted field research in Hunan Province, China. Were there any unforgettable experiences you could share with us?

There were indeed many great experiences, but let me share some of the most memorable ones. First, I went to regions I had never been to before in China. My parents' hometown is Wenzhou, and we would often visit either that city or other large coastal cities. My research in Hunan allowed me to discover much more about Chinese culture and history, and to get a better appreciation for its inestimable diversity.

In addition, while designing the script, it strengthened the ideas I have about type design: it is not only about shapes, but also about the culture behind the characters. There is a unique bond between a culture and its language that cannot be ignored. Designing a typeface in a script that is not familiar to the designer is possible, but he or she has to be aware that there exists a fragile line between an ugly typeface and a creative typeface in the eyes of the users, and this is not something that the non-native designer can decide definitively.

Nüshu script is a syllabic script. Did this cause any difficulties in the design of Nüshu typeface? How did you solve the problem?

As the samples displayed in the Unicode Standard tables are the results of the extensive research (led by Professor Liming Zhao with her linguists team from Tsinghua University in Beijing), I could refer to the 396 glyphs from this same table with confidence, without necessarily having to learn how to read or write those glyphs.

However, as these glyphs are a selection of the most used ones based on this research, there were from time to time a few glyphs that couldn't be found in the table, or with various degrees of differences from the samples in the Unicode table. Besides the visual differences, Nüshu works on a syllabic system as you mentioned, so when I had a doubt about a glyph's appearance, I could still rely on a couple of Nüshu-Chinese dictionaries!

What do you think about the possible impact on type design and Nüshu culture as a result of giving Nüshu a digital presence?

I don't think this project would have a huge impact on type design industry. But it can at least be a reminder that type design has strong cultural backgrounds.

As for Nüshu culture, I think that Noto Sans Nüshu can make some contribution to the effort to keep the culture alive, as it opens up the possibility of writing texts in Nüshu script on digital media and sharing messages on many devices, which is vital in this digital era. Hopefully even better, there will be other designers who would involved in making Nüshu typefaces!

Noto Sans Nüshu

BLUE BELT—ADVANCED COMPREHENSION AND SKILLS

5

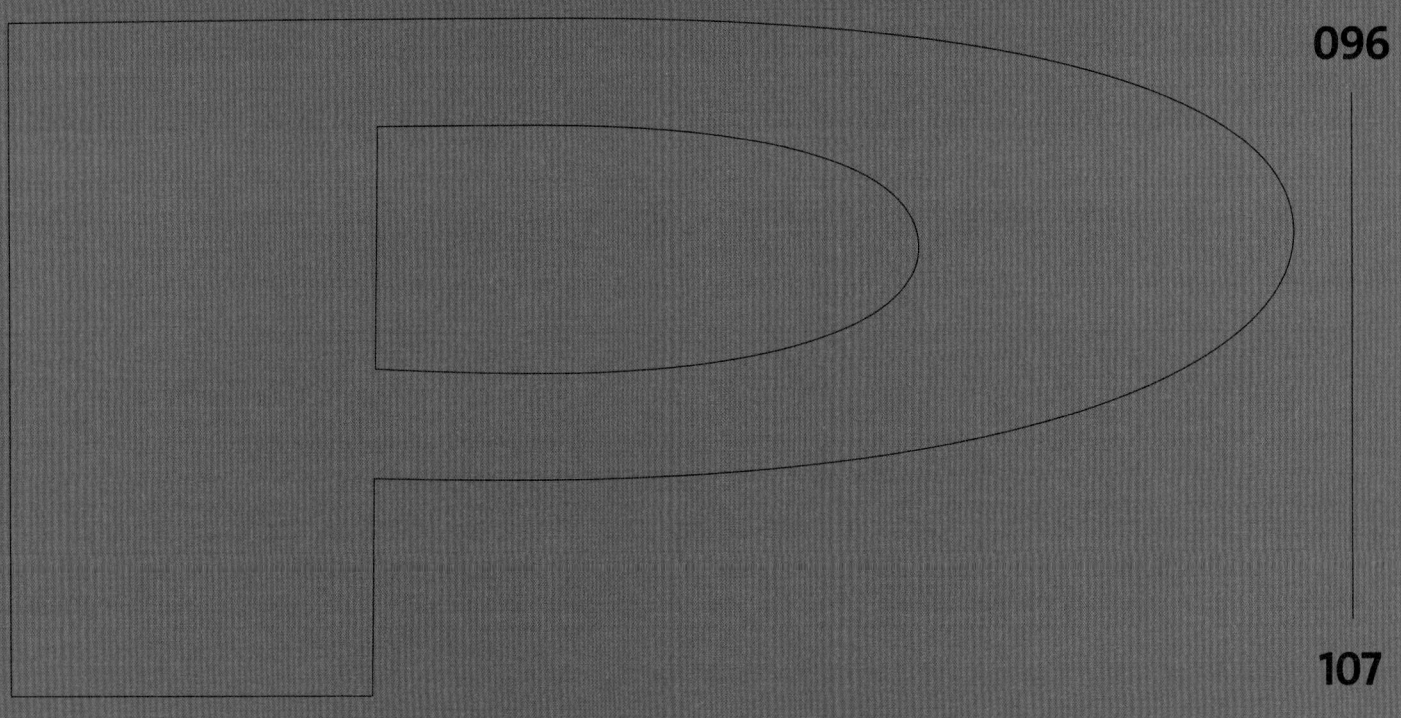

096-107

An excellent typographer can select suitable typefaces that suit the temperament of the work based on content, layout, visual requirements and other factors, so that the typeface can better accentuate the quality of the work. This kind of appropriate selection is based on typographer's accumulated experiences and practices. As for judo, the brown belt is the penultimate step for judokas before the ultimate goal of black belt. This ranking requires judokas to be able to flexibly use a range of techniques according to various practical situations.

CROSSING BOUNDARIES, BREAKING RULES

Editor
Gal

"...can be accomplished without principles." Human behavior is complex and varied, ... moving forward in an orderly way from a macro perspective. Human behavior cannot ... role played by codes of conduct in regulating and restraining people's actions and impulses. ... there to various rules in daily life, such as traffic rules, school rules, business regulations, and so on. ... are one of the ways that social stability and security are maintained. However, sometimes, rules can be ... in some fields.

Unlike physics, mathematics and other fields where there exist standard answers, there is no single answer in the ... design. There can be 100 different ways for 100 different designers to achieve the best visual effects, and their ... spire completely opposite and conflicting responses depending on the audience. It is because of the ... involved in the design process that any thoughts on requiring designers to follow a common set ... them to wrap themselves up in a creative strait-jacket. As Yoshihisa Shirai, the famous ... view, "Traditional book format design, after all, is only a guideline for reference,

... mat design. He is active in the fields of book and magazine, editing and p... ... of the design of *IDEA* magazine as Art Director and designer, he has also ... as *Tadanori Yokoo Complete Book Designs*, Mishima Tentou's collection of ... ects. Being well versed in book format design, Shirai has a clear position ... grid system—they are all merely guidelines for reference. He argues that ... search through and choose appropriate proportions and structures for ... urpose of layout design is not about following guidelines, but rather about ... " At the same time, Shirai pays great attention to the combinations of Japa... to present a unified and harmonious visual effect through font combinat... to act as a coordinator between different scripts, finding the common tempera...

Shirai advocates a design philosophy—having rules, while ... ules. A rule, sometimes, is like a mirror, which can reflect the part that people still need to impro... rule is just like an imaginary line, and one may gain unexpected surprises after crossing that line. It's j... ne colors a coloring book, and occasionally draws outside of the line. Perhaps it is this transgression—the par... painted outside the line, which could become the distinctive personal trait of the creator.

Dialogue with YOSHIHISA SHIRAI

Yoshihisa Shirai

A prestigious Japanese graphic designer specializing in book design and editorial design. Shirai is well known as the Art Director of the magazine *IDEA*. He also works as a professor in the Visual Communication Design Department of Musashino Art University.

Interviewers
Siyun He & Wanting Zeng

DON'T BE RESTRAINED BY THE RULES

Q&A

For beginners in graphic design, what kind of knowledge is necessary for selecting fonts?

First of all, it is necessary to understand basically what is a body text font and what is a display font. Then, choose a font you are interested in from the many fonts and try to use it to see its visual effect. When you do that, you are supposed to learn when, where, and for what purpose the font was created, and who created it.

As Jan Tschichold said, when we get to know a font, we unavoidably know the fonts related to it, such as the fonts influenced by it, the fonts that influenced it, similar fonts, its contemporary fonts, and other fonts created by the same designer, all of which makes our understanding of the font more comprehensive.

In book design, the choice of text typeface immensely affects reading experience. Do you have any preferable text typefaces? What aspects do you value most when you choose?

Basically, the fonts chosen should match the text content in terms of form and functionality. However, it is worth noting that even the selection prioritizing form and functionality does not necessarily mean that it is adapting to the text content.

Other selection criteria include the era when the font was produced, the country or region where it was produced, and its intended purpose. Apart from that, the selected font may also reflect the author's personality, his or her desired atmosphere (gentle, soft, calm, tough, etc.), or the meaning the author wants to deliver beyond the text itself.

In my case, I try not to choose a font based on my own preference. However, when I look back on my works, I find that my selected fonts show more "bias" than I thought. Surprising things like that often happen.

You once said in an interview that book format is just a guideline, and a Western book format cannot be directly applied to Japanese typography. A book format with good readability requires designers to have their own analysis and thinking. What is good readability like? Does it have any design standards?

The concept, proportion of book format, was first proposed by William Morris, then inherited by Edward Johnston, and integrated by Jan Tschichold. In the late 1940s, the grid system was introduced and advocated by Joseph Müller Brockmann and other graphic designers. These have become the commonly acknowledged methodologies and ideas as standards for ideal print on paper design. However, they only represent reference values as a guideline instead of rules. Through analyzing and trying out these guidelines, designers will develop a better understanding.

Book format design is a dynamic process combining flexible utilization and application of those standards, while seeking the appropriate proportion and structure of each text. It requires a grasp of the sequence, hierarchy, and structure of the texts on the page, and an analysis of the relationship between different units based on categories such as book unit, feature as well as spread, and, lastly, to organically integrate all of the elements as a whole.

In terms of Japanese typography, the first issue to be addressed is to choose a vertical or horizontal writing mode, because that decision may lead to a totally different layout structure. And using the horizontal writing mode does not mean that the book format of Western texts is completely applicable, because despite the fact that two directions are available for Japanese typography, Japanese characters were originally designed as a vertical-axis structure adapting to the vertical arrangement. Thus, when designers set Japanese characters one next to another, compared to Latin text, Japanese text blocks have a narrower width and a larger line space.

Book format is a functional structure encompassing character space, line space, column space, and column width based on reason, while its arrangement of printed and non-printed areas is directed by the visual sense.

Even a well-designed book format may not be suitable for all designs, it is not necessary to stick with the standardized norms when there are images and text that don't match. The purpose of layout design is not about following the guidelines, but about providing reader-friendly text and images.

I think a typographic design that is able to incorporate the sensational and the rational, verbal and written expression, and that relates to what the text is saying, is ideal. Good readability is not exclusively contributed by typographic designers but is also a collaboration with readers.

Bilingual typography is a challenge that graphic designers from all over the world are faced with. In your working experience, have you had difficulties in using Japanese and Latin typefaces together in layouts? How did you address them?

In the last decade, foundries creating Latin and Japanese typefaces have launched one solution after another to address the issues of multilingual or Japanese and Latin mixed text composition. Many of these have been solved by the curent Desktop Publishing. In the past, designers had to adjust type size for the selected Japanese and Latin fonts, but this is no longer needed thanks to the technology of composite fonts.

However, due to the great discrepancy between Japanese script and the Latin alphabet, as well as Japanese script and East Asian writing systems (simplified Chinese, traditional Chinese, Korean, etc.), it is extremely difficult to align these scripts in terms of form, style, and density. That is not only because Japanese has its own complicated lingual structure (a hybrid of Chinese characters, hiragana, katakana, numeralsm Latin letters, punctuation marks, etc.), but the formal and structural differences between Asian and Western scripts are huge.

Thus, we need to design on the premise of the acceptance of the difference and get rid of the constraints cast by the ideas of modern design—try to find the essence of communication shared by the two scripts and convey this essence.

You attach great importance to the rules of Japanese-Latin mixed typography, but you also advocate the idea of respecting and breaking the rules at the same time. Can you explain and give some examples of which rules should be stuck to and which can be broken?

For a designer who needs to work on multilingual typographic composition, I think it is important to bear respect for all writing systems. Understanding texts of different languages requires the assistance of linguistic experts. Similarly, typographic composition with different texts needs support from typographic experts in different writing systems.

The emphasis does not lie in breaking typographic norms, because book format, after all, is only a guideline for reference, rather than a set of rules. The purpose of typographic design is to communicate with readers. If placing the content in the grid makes the page look rigid—as if it has no air to breathe—then you can open the door called grid and let fresh air flow in, so that breathing can be easier.

What is the most difficult problem you have encountered so far in layout design? Is there anything that confuses you currently?

Difficulties are the most common things in layout design, however, they are also the charm of it. What challenges me is to make my design a commercial success. A good design is not necessarily a hot sale product. Similarly, a best-selling design is not necessarily a good design. It would not be so difficult if design was only about style and idea.

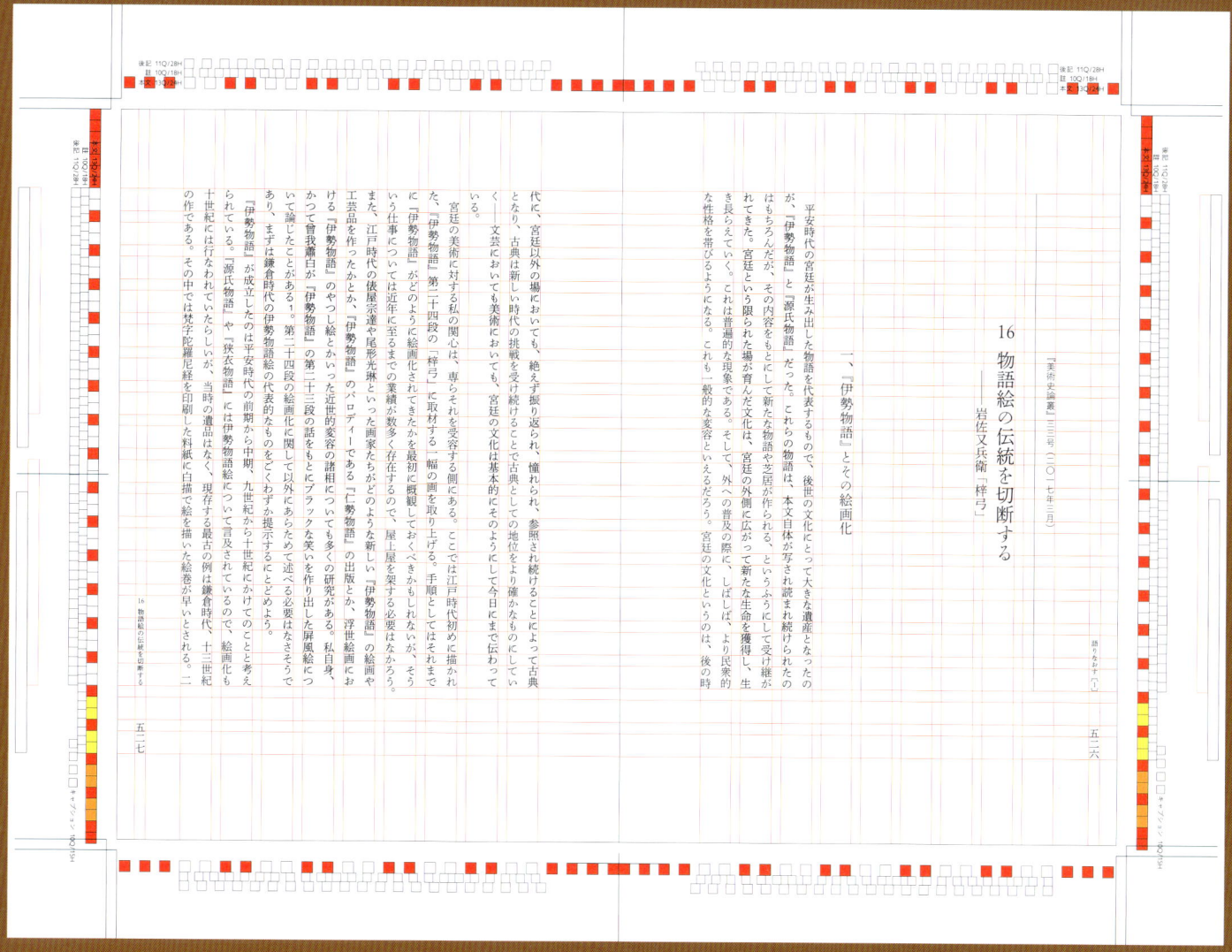

絵は語り始めるだろうか: Sato Yasuhiro, published by Hatori Shoten, 2018

You once mentioned that you started by learning the Swiss style and gradually developed a Japanese typographic style. And now, Japanese style has become a quite unique, widely acknowledged, and mature style in the world. From your perspective, what is the uniqueness of the Japanese typographic style compared with the Western?

When I was in my twenties, I admired the methodology and style of the Swiss design style (International design) and aimed to apply it to Japanese typography. Over time, however, my design style naturally has been influenced by Japanese culture and customs, just as my life has. Admittedly, Japanese as a linguistic system is a Japanese design style in itself: Japanese first introduced Chinese characters, developed hiragana and katakana on the basis of Chinese characters, and then brought in Arabic numerals and Latin letters. Japanese text is a hybrid of many different elements.

As far as I am concerned, much so-called Japanese style phenomena and forms are not actually unique to Japan. By the same token, I am also deeply convinced that those things that have been imported into Japan from China and the West have been transformed by Japanese influences. So, personally, I do not see any essential differences between Japanese and Western designs, and I have never perceived the two in isolation.

But, if there is anything that distinguishes Japan from the West (or China), I think it is the Japanese consciousness of language. Japanese were originally a race that did not have a writing system and lived in a climate that did not require it. In other words, compared with the people living in the mainland, Japanese consciousness of written text (to record and convey, or leave symbols and words) was weaker. From my perspective, such consciousness also reflects on design, doesn't it?

ローマン体活字の開花

「再生」とか「文芸復興」と呼ばれるルネサンスが、14世紀中頃にイタリアを中心として湧き起こりました。中世の宗教から人間を開放し、人間の自由と個人の独立と権利を主張して、ギリシャとローマの古典を読み直し、新たに解釈をしようとする精神的な運動でした。その推進なったのが、人文主義者（ヒューマニスト）たちでした。彼らは、語学を愛し、古典作品の収集や研究を通じて、現実的な人間精神を謳歌し、著作（古典や聖書の注釈書）を多く残しました。彼らが用いた文字の書体は、当時一般であったブラック・レターではなく、キャロリン・ミナスキュールズを洗練させた読み易い書風でした。

ルネサンスの花が咲きほこっていたイタリアに、初めて印刷術を紹介したのは、マインツから来た、スウェインハイムとパナルツという2人の印刷者でした。彼らは1465年にローマ近郊のスビアコという町に印刷所を設け、ブラック・レターをやや明るく丸く改良した、人文主義者手書きの書体を活字化して印刷しました。

この2人が1467年にローマに移ると、ドイツ人ウルリク・ハンもローマに入り、1468年に先の2人の活字をやや改良した書体を使って印刷しました。

1469年にはドイツ人のダ・スピラ兄弟（ヨハンとウェンデリン）が、ヴェニスにおいてハンの活字よりもベースライン・セリフを意識して様式化の進んだ活字を用いました。

そして1470頃になると、スウェインハイムとパナルツの活字を彫ったと推定されている、フランス人のニコラ・ジェンソン（1420—80）が、北イタリアの人文主義者の手書き書体をモデルにして、ハンやスピラたちの活字よりもいっそう洗練された、読み易い明るい書体をヴェニスにおいて設計しました。ここにおいてローマン体活字が、ドイツ風の黒く重く威圧するブラック・レターを離れて、新しい書体として登場しました。この書体はヒューマニスト系（またはヴェネチアン系）と呼ばれ、ローマン体の元祖とされています。

14—15世紀に四ノ方との貿易で最も栄えていたヴェニス共和国は、東地中海を領地として、東方貿易を独占しました。15世紀中頃にトルコがギリシャを占領したことにより、ギリシャ人の難民がヴェニスに移り住み、古代ギリシャの文献（写本）が持ち込まれ、人文主義者たちがゆの文献を求めて、多勢このヴェニスを中心に古典の研究に熱中していました。

一二三四五六七八九十一二三四五六七八九十一二三四五六七八九十一二三四五六七八九十一二三四五六七八九十一二三四五六七八九十一二三四五六七八九十一二三四五六七八九十一二三四五六七八九十ギリシャ語の写本が入手しやすいヴェニスで、ギリシャ語の書物を印刷することを思いついて、この地に1490年頃印刷所を開いたのは、アルドゥス・マニティウス（1450—1515）です。彼はギリシャ人の学者や、ヨーロッパ各国の人文主義者を集めて、編集・執筆・校正・印刷・出版の事業をひとりで運営し、人文主義者たちの需要に応え、成功を収めました。

アルドゥスが出版の総合小見出し

プロデューサーとしてタイポグラフィ上に与えた影響は、以下の3つにまとめられます。

その第1は、ギリシャ語の活字化に挑み、古典を多数出版し、新興中産階級層に売り込んだことです。この活字は、多種のアクセントや合字や連語や短縮語が使われています。アルドゥス工房で働いていたギリシャ人学者の、手書き書体を活字化したといわれています。

a. Uncial　マタイの福音書にみるアンシャルの例です。
ペンはまっすぐにゆっくり動き、そのため優美な印象をあたえます。（8世紀　パリ）
b. Later Roman Cursive　新しいローマのイタリック。

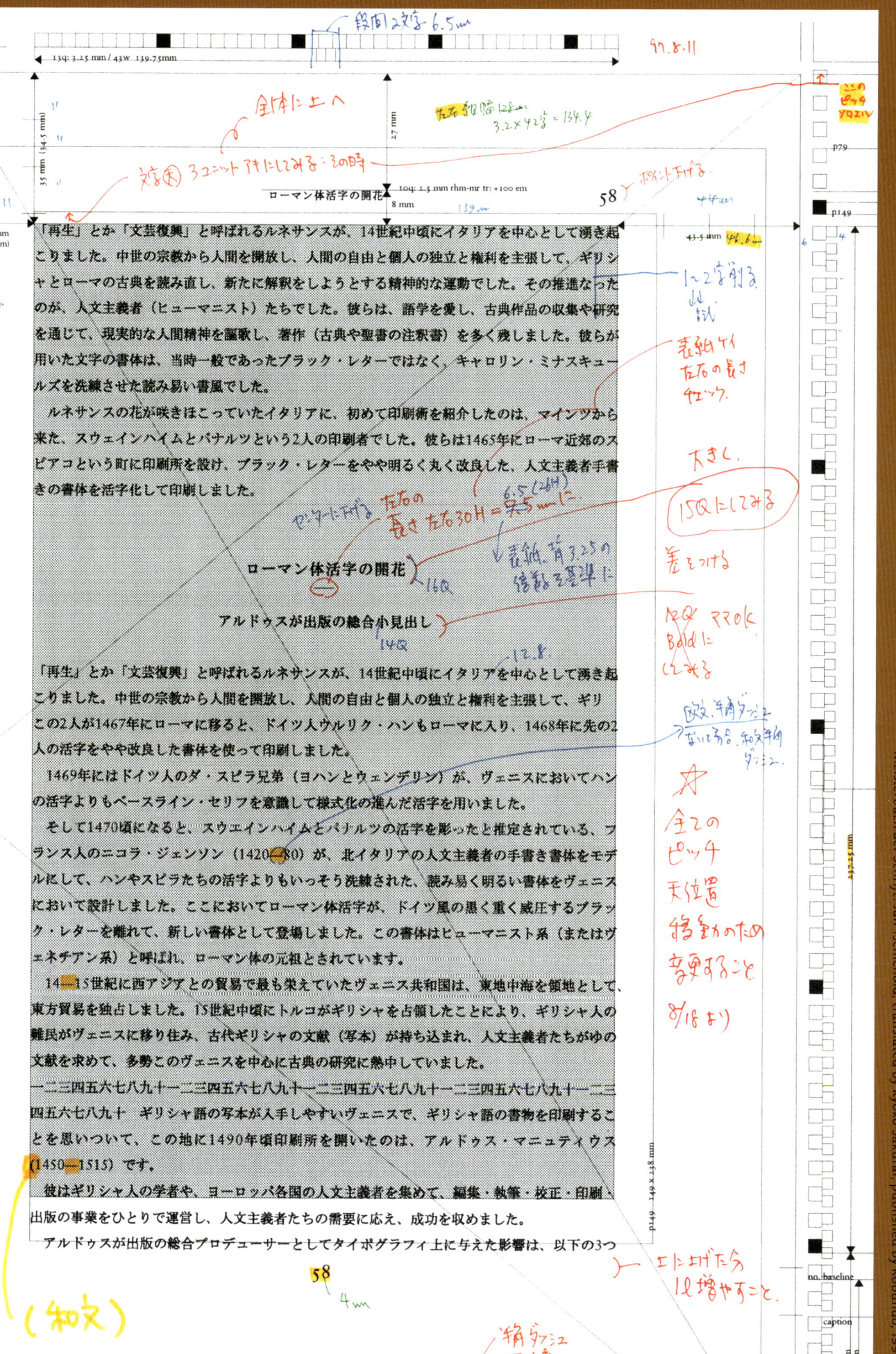

ABCDEFGHIJKLM
NOPQRSTUVWXYZ
abcdefghijklmnop
qrstuvwxyz æœfifl
0123456789
!?&(){}[]''""‚„.,:;--*

Template Gothic

掲載されたことで、それは芸術センターの人気を確かなものにする手助けとなった。アカデミックな教育の場や芸術の世界の自由さは、形態を思うがままに扱って実験することを可能にし、こうした土壌から革新的な形態が生まれる。商業的な利害関係に影響されるメインストリームは、より慎重で、そのために目新しい形態に貪欲だ。

メインストリームの作品は、過去からも形態を盗用する。ポストモダニズムの表明であれ、一部のデザイナーの創造性の枯渇による怠惰であれ、「長過ぎる期間、デザイン史は、盗作可能なスタイルの見本市として扱われてきた。」(キャサリン・マッコイ、1990年) 歴史的なムーブメントの表層の意味を剥ぎ取って再利用することは、今日の実体を欠いたイメージの失墜をさらに拡大させる。10年という括りが、主にその様式によって定義されるようになるにつれ、歴史は過度に簡略化され、ゆがめられ、その複雑さは誤って認識される。現代のアメリカのデザイナー、ポーラ・シェアの回顧展の告知に、ロシア構成主義の形態を使うことはアメリカ文化全体の歴史認識に対する無知をさらに拡げるものだ。なぜなら既に旧い手法である以上に、実際のところ両者を通じた接点など存在しないからである。実在する出来事、実在する事件、実在する生、死、戦争、哲学、そして理想は、一連のスタイリスティックな記号表現へと行き着き、それは利用可能なイメージの貯蔵庫へと流れ込み、商品を売るために使用される時を待っている。

個人の様式：スターデザイナーの地位と落とし穴

個性的な独自のスタイルを持ち成功しているデザイナーが言うように、影響力と剽窃とを分けるラインは限りなく不明瞭かもしれない。ネヴィル・ブロディの初期の自由闊達な、ボールド体とジオメトリックなサンセリフ体を用いていた『ザ・フェイス』誌の誌面の特徴的な仕事から、最近の『アリーナ』誌の仕事に見られる、余計なものを省き、Helveticaとグリッドを基準にしてページをデザインするというスタイルへの変化は、必要から生じた結果である。彼の初期のスタイルは一目瞭然で、独特な個性を持っていたが、彼の作品をユニークなものにするスタイリスティックな表現は、同時に容赦なく「進化し続ける新しいもの」を追求するなかで、簡単に盗用されてしまうものだった。この消費と盗用の一歩先を行くために、彼は自分のスタイルをまったく新しいところから見直す必要があったのだ。

デザイナーは、スタイルのパラドックスに捕われている。一目瞭然な独特のスタイルは簡単に盗用されるが、同時に、もっとも良く認識され、評価され、出版物に掲載されるものでもある。エイプリル・グライマンのスタイルは、特定のクライアントの要請にではなく彼女の個人的な成長の過程と、より直接的に対応している。彼女の知名度は、その仕事に対しての妥当性でも、彼女のデザインの解法の本質的な正当性によるものでも、作品の機能によるものでもなく、彼女のスタイルによるものだ。

グラフィックデザインは必ずしも儲かる職業ではないことから、多くのデザイナーにとってデザイン業界における知名度が見返りとなり自己満足が重要となる。しかし作品のスタイルがとらえにくいものであったり、それを理解するために、解読や熱心な取組みや、最悪の場合「時間」が必要であったり、忙しくてデザイナーが作品をユニークなものにする作業に取りかかる暇がなかったりした場合、仕事に対しての見返りを得ることのできる表面的な評価の体系のお世話になることができない可能性が高い。皮肉にも、マーケティングの忠実な下僕として働くデザイナーたち (正真正銘の機能主義者たちだ!) についても同じことが言える。彼らは大概は、カメレオンのようにその作品の背後に隠れているから匿名のままなのだ。

グラフィックデザインにとってはスタイルがすべてだ。クライアントから要求された「課題」に形態と表層とを適用することだ。すべては「適用すること」につきる。現代社会においてデザイナーは、クライアントの選択においてのみ、そのデザイナーの内なる声を表明することができる。グラフィックデザインのコラボレーションにおいて個性的なスタイルを仕事に当てはめるためには、機能主義者の「初めにクライアントがあり、クライアントが課題を決定する」という手法とは逆に、個々のスタイルにふさわしいクライアントを見つけることだ。ネヴィル・ブロディがファッションや出版に関わる分野の仕事を手がけ、エイプリル・グライマンが建築家やアカデミックな世界やブティックの仕事を請け負い、ポール・ランドが企業のために働くように。

すべてのデザイナーが、あらゆるデザイン上の課題に取り組めるようになることを期待するのは無理な話である。2人のデザイナーがまったく同じ「デザイン的な解法」を提示することなど決してあり得ないことからもわかるように、デザイナーは独自のスタイル、もしくは個人的な趣向から抜け出すことはできない。視覚的な形態の持つ意味が、一過性のものであると認めるのであれば、私たちの作り出す形態のスタイルは、文化の変容にともなって (私たちの発想やプロセスや価値観が変わるにしろ変わらないにしろ)、またデザイナーとしてのキャリアを踏まえて (個人の範囲のなかで) 流動的に適切な答えを出していかなくてはならない。「その形態は最近はもう使っていないのです。今の私が試みていることとは可読性の概念に注目するものです。可読性に関するあなたの論文の内容は、私の最近の仕事のことのように思えましたよ。なぜならデザインの歴史の連続性を全体的に俯瞰した大きな文脈を踏まえそえで、これまで私個人が一貫してとってきたスタイルと、そこでの論点は重なっていますから。」というわけだろうか？ おそらくそうは言えないだろう。それが実際は本当っぽいとしても。ワインガルトやジョナサン・バーンブルク、あるいはスコロス・ウェデルの作品は、他のデザイナーたちに向けたスライド発表やデザイン年鑑、あるいはデザイン関係の出版物それぞれの文脈を踏まえて、まずはそのつくり手自身に、次にデザイナーたちに、最後に想定された読者に対して訴えかけてきたものだからだ。

連続体

「様式は私たちをいっそう隔てるが、イデオロギーは普遍的な視野で私たちを結びつける」

(ダン・フリードマン、1991年)

目新しい形態に貪欲な「ネオマニア」の絶え間ない消費の圧力が、物事を前へと進めていく動機となる本当の意味での発展と革新の必要性を失墜させることのないように願っている。直線的な進化と進歩の概念は、西洋文化に固有のものである。デザインの歴史の連続体は、新しい一歩がその前の一歩を超えていくことが進歩であると往々にして誤解されてきた。この単線的な進歩史観は、可能性の極点もしくは究極の答えを目指す飽くなき上昇志向を内包している。

マッシモ・ヴィネッリのような一部のデザイナーは、その究極の目的地としてのモダニズムに固執している。「広大な歴史的観点から見た場合でも、モダニズムの禁欲主義的で質実剛健なスタイルは、力強さと品格を兼ね備えた傑出した地点にある。一過性の価値観に対してモダニズムの持つ不朽の価値観は、いまだに私に知的刺激を与えつづけてくれる。」おそらく初期のモダニストの普遍性の探究とスイスのモダニストの不朽のデザインの追求とが、約束の地へと辿り着くことを待ち望み続けてきたアメリカのデザインの糧となっているのだろう。

しかし辞書によれば、連続体とは「同一の構成要素による切れ間なく続く連続」と定義されている。文脈と価値観が移り行く中で、グラフィックデザインが出す答えもまた絶えず変化する。それぞれの新しいステップは必ずしもより優れているのではなく、ただ異なり、同時に先行する仕事への返答でもあり、新しい社会環境をつくりだしていく文化の影響力の現れなのだ。個々のスターデザイナーに注目するデザイン史によって失われ、デザインコンペとその結果としてのデザイン年鑑の中で失われてしまった個別の文脈が、グラフィックデザインの制作と分析にとっては極めて重要なのである。

表層は移り変わる。形態に隠された意味は、絶え間ない変化の中にある。今日の世俗的状況を把握し続けるためには、発展と、思考の新たな展開、もしくは少なくとも思考範囲を拡げていくことが必要とされる。思考と形態は上下の軸となる文脈と、左右の軸となる連続体の中で形成される。ワインガルトの手法と、その反抗精神、そして直感的な意思決定は今でも共鳴できるものがある。しかし、彼の形式的語彙（フォーマル・ボキャブラリー）は燃え盛るような勢いを失ってしまったのである。それに対して、キャサリン・マッコイは彼女のデザインの職業倫理に欠かすことのできない揺るぎない信念を保ちつつ、形態を進化させていくことに成功した。彼女は言語学の理論や、ヴァナキュラー（土着的）なものの斬新なとらえ方、MTVやフォトショップなど、新しい影響力を前向きに取り入れた。彼女の形式的語彙は広く、変化し、その作品は常に新鮮さを失わない。アイデアは（時代を超えるとまでは言わないが）より持久性があるが、形態の寿命は次第に短くなっていっている。形式的語彙は、外的および内的な刺激に呼応する変化に対して前向きでなくてはならないのである。

だとすれば、今日私たちに課せられた目標は「ネオマニア」の影響を受け入れることではなく、その現実に果敢に取り組むことだ。常に変遷し続ける文化が美学的な環境、またデザイン業界内に閉塞した価値体系の双方に与えるインパクトを理解し、モダニストの思想が及ぼした影響の数々を認め、個々の美意識とスタイルの支配力、そして事実上、仕事の表層的な側面ばかりを扱う内輪誉めばかりの業界体質を見直すことだ。これらの現実を認めることは、より良い答えを追求することでもある。この答えは、時間とともに変化していくものでもある。それゆえにあまり包括的また具体的すぎず、普遍的な答えではなく、個々の関心により結びついたものであることが望ましい。イデオロギーに対する、より多元的な視点を持ち、美学への関心を蔑むのではなく受容することが、理論と実践の現実的な結びつきを可能にするのだ。

文化人類学者は、文化の内部と外部の両方に所属することのやっかいさをよく知っている。なぜならば文化人類学者は、観察者としてフィールドワークを行う際、観察される側の領域内部に身を置きつつ、同時に一歩離れた立場を貫かなければならないからである。文化人類学者にとっては、この観察者としての立場がジレンマである。文化人類学を研究する意義は、異文化を研究することで自らの文化を考察する、あるいはリベラル・ヒューマニズム的な言い回しを借りるならば、「他者を知ることで己をよりよく知る」ということだ。しかしながら、観察する側とされる側との力関係は必然的に偏るために、両者の関係が中立的になることはあり得ない。グラフィックデザイナーもまた同様のジレンマを抱えている——グラフィックデザイナーは文化の産物をつくり出す存在でありながら、同時にその産物が流通している社会の一員でもある。また、グラフィックデザイナーはしばしば、自分個人の社会的立場や経験から離れて、職業的なヴィジュアル・コミュニケーションの専門家として活動することが要請される。このような"職業化"あるいは"専門化"と呼ばれるような切り離しによって、デザインの制作過程における、完全に自律的で客観的な観察者という神秘的な立場がつくり出される。これは職業的に必要なやり方だとされ、あらゆるグラフィックデザインの方法論の根幹をなす"問題解決"のための、欠かせない作法だとされる。私たちグラフィックデザイナーは客観的であることを求められ、合理的な判断（あるいは解決法）を導き出すことが期待されている。また、そうすることではじめて、グラフィックデザインは他の様々な職能と同等の地位にあるとされる。もちろん、グラフィックデザイナーも社会の構成員であり、他のデザイナーがつくり出したもの、さらに自らがつくり出したものに囲まれて生きている。このように、グラフィックデザイナーは自らの文化の外部（や周辺）に身を置くと同時に、自らがその文化の一部であるプロフェッショナルであることを求められるのだ。

社会の他の構成員と同じく私たちグラフィックデザイナーもまた、文化の産物をめぐる消費活動の観察者であると同時に参加者でもあり、これらの文化的産物に誘惑されたり、嫌悪感を抱いたりといった感情を分かち合う。私は他者のメッセージに魅惑されている——美しい書物の物質的な魅力に惹かれ、政治的なポスターの切迫感に圧倒され、そして、ショッピングセンターで買い物をする。私は他者からのメッセージによって突き動かされる——不正な行いに憤然とし、憎悪の感情に恐怖し、そしてまた、ショッピングセンターで買い物をする。この告白から教訓とするべきは、文化的な産物の消費とそれが発するメッセージの受け取り方は人さまざまであるということである。これまで文化的な産物の消費活動においては、どのようなメッセージにも反応する白紙状態の消費者が想定されてきた。ところが近年の研究は、この受け手の消費者像に別の見方を示している。私たちはちょっとした行動を通じた個人レベルでの抵抗行動によって、象徴的に、ときには風刺的に文化の産物を消費しているのである。私はテレビドラマ「メルローズ・プレイス」の、いかにもメロドラマ的な筋書きや陳腐な芝居をそうと分かった上で観る。そのダメでいかにもな感じがいいのである。その一方で、ケーブルテレビへの加入は断固拒否している。そんなにたくさんのチャンネルはいらないからだ。

内と外：
デザインの文化と
文化のデザイン

アンドリュー・ブラウベルト

In and Around:
Cultures of Design
and
the Design of Cultures

by *Andrew Blauvelt*

著者アンドリュー・ブラウベルトはミネアポリスにあるウォーカー・アートセンターのデザイン・ディレクターである。
本文は1994年『エミグレ』第32号にて発表された。

082

- マーティン・F・ルクルトは民法の公証人として働く一方で、国際的なポスターコレクターとして知られる。20世紀のグラフィックデザインとポスターについての著作多数。

  Martijn F. Le Coultre is by profession a civil-law notary who for a hobby collects international posters. He has written many books and essays on the subject of 20th-century graphic arts and poster design.

- アルストン・W・パービスはボストン大学美術校のグラフィックデザイン科教授。グラフィックデザイン関連の多くの著作の執筆にも携わる。

  Alston W. Purvis is Chairman of the Graphic Design Department at the Boston University College of Fine Arts and the author of numerous publications on graphic design.

破壊されたが、ハーバート・マターを初めとするデザイナーのポスターを含むチヒョルト自身の収集品の大部分は、幸運にも、ナチ時代を生き延びた。沢山の蔵書類は1933年のナチによる捜査の際に失われてしまったが、多くの研究資料はミュンヘンのマイスター訓練校に保管されていた。チヒョルトは機を失せずにドイツを離れられたので、自身の作品、所有していたモンドリアンの絵画、バウハウスの家具類などは失わずに済んだ。

1930年代にチヒョルトはニューヨークの近代美術館（MoMA）と接触を持ち、美術館はチヒョルトを通じて数々の物品をコレクションに加えている。その中にはチヒョルトの作品と並んでマン・レイやリシツキーの作品があった。1950年、チヒョルトは同美術館の建築とデザイン部門の創設者である建築家フィリップ・ジョンソンを通じて、彼の集めたポスター作品やその他の応用美術作品の残りも同美術館に売却した。チヒョルトの死後、彼の書簡の多くはカリフォルニア、ロサンジェルスに拠点をおくゲッティ一研究所が購入した。またバーゼルやチューリヒの美術館、ミュンヘンの「ノイエ・ザンムルング」にもチヒョルトは作品の一部を残している。

1941年のスイス国籍取得から1974年にロカルノ近くのベルツォーナで亡くなるまで、チヒョルトはデザイナー、著述家として活躍を続けた。「新しいタイポグラフィ」の主導的提唱者として、モダニストのグラフィックデザインにチヒョルトがなした貢献は恒久不変で、しかも多面的である。また伝統的タイポグラフィ再興の唱導者として、チヒョルトは書籍デザインに人文主義の伝統を回復させるための主要な原動力ともなった。彼が後世のグラフィックデザイナーに与えるであろう影響は、当時においても計り知れないと思われていた。著述、教育、そして自らのタイポグラフィを通じ、チヒョルトは「新しいタイポグラフィ」の原理のみならず、ロシア構成主義やバウハウスの原理を普及することにも一役買った。

高名な米国のグラフィックデザイナー、ポール・ランドはイギリスの雑誌「コマーシャルアート」の1930年7月号の記事、「印刷のなかの新しい生活」を通じてチヒョルトに出会った。その記事は「新しいタイポグラフィ」のためにチヒョルトが書いた序文の英訳であった。この序文に大いに触発されたランドは、ツヴァルト、シュヴィッタース、リシツキー、ブルフハルツ、サトナー、デクセル、モホリ＝ナジのようなモダニストのグラフィックデザイナーを意識するようになった。ランドは「プリント」誌の1969年1月号でチヒョルトを回顧した際、多くのグラフィックデザイナーに向けて次のように述べている。「タイポグラフィとはどんなふうに見られようとも、困難、精妙かつ厄介な技芸であることに変わりありません。ある程度の技法的熟練までは誰もが共有できるとしても、タイポグラフィの免許皆伝は眼力の優れた人のだけの領分であり、ごく少数だけが辿り着ける特権的なものなのです。」

彼のヴィジョン

彼の感受性の鋭さ

彼の献身

タイポグラフィの開拓者

自らの技の主人となった人

タイポグラフィの歴史家

教えてくれた新しきものへの意識，

古きものへの尊敬

我らに残したSaskiaとSabonに

我らを導いた比類なき精妙と洗練に

彼の総合に，抑制に，資質に

私は彼，ヤン・チヒョルトを讃える。*7

［訳：小田部麻利子］

*7 Gottschall, p. 43. Paul Rand, *Print Magazine*, January 1969

no in 1974. As the leading propagandist of the New Typography his contributions to modernist graphic design are both permanent and manifold, and as an advocate of a revival of traditional typography he was a major force in restoring a humanist tradition to book design. His influence on future graphic designers was incalculable. Through his writing, teaching, and his own typography, Tschichold not only spread the principles of the New Typography but also those of Russian constructivism and the Bauhaus.

The eminent American graphic designer Paul Rand was introduced to Tschichold through an article titled "A New Life in Print" in the July 1930 issue of the British journal *Commercial Art*, a translation of Tschichold's introduction to *Die Neue Typographie*. This greatly inspired Rand and made him aware of modernist graphic designers such as Zwart, Schwitters, Lissitsky, Burchartz, Sutnar, Dexel, and Moholy-Nagy. Rand spoke for many graphic designers when he reflected on Tschichold in the January 1969 issue of *Print Magazine*: "Typography, no matter how it is looked at, remains a difficult, subtle, and exacting art. And even though a certain degree of technical skill is relatively common, typographic mastery is the province of the perceptive and the prerogative of the few."

"For his vision,

his sensitivity

and his dedication,

for being a pioneer typographer,

a master of his craft

and a typographic historian,

for teaching us awareness of the

new and respect for the old,

for giving us Saskia and Sabon,

for pointing out those subtleties

and refinements without which

we would be the poorer,

for his integrity, his restraint,

and for his quality,

I salute Jan Tschichold."*7

111

BLACK BELT — PROFESSIONAL SHOWCASE

A Activity

ŚWIDNICKI FESTIWAL FILMOWY SPEKTRUM

AD & D
Krzysztof Ignasiak &
Marcin Matuszak

DS
Bekarty

2019

MALTA FESTIVAL 2017/
THE BALKANS PLATFORM

AD & D
Krzysztof Ignasiak &
Marcin Matuszak

DS
Bekarty

2017

The identity of the Malta Festival Poznań 2017 comprised five slogans: We, the People; We, the Balkans; We, the East; We, Europe; We, Others.
Each can be interpreted in two ways. The first underlines the unity and homogeneity of the subject it refers to; and the second, on the contrary, juxtaposes the two subjects and suggests their polarity. The first makes a generalization and the second arbitrarily delineates borders. Both philosophy and experience suggested to many that these slogans not only did not work, but also actively posed a danger. This is why designers openly crossed them out.

BLACK BELT — PROFESSIONAL SHOWCASE

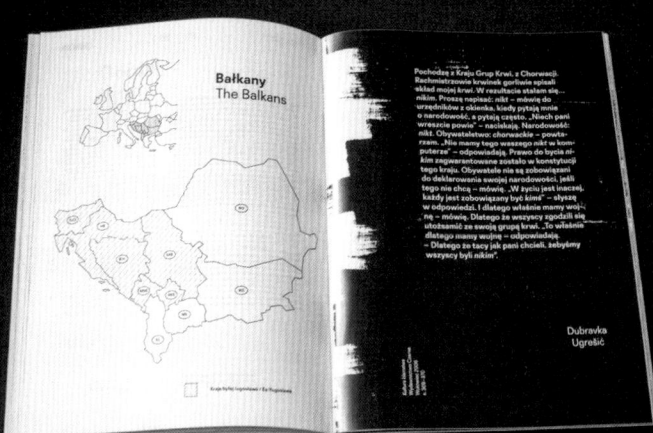

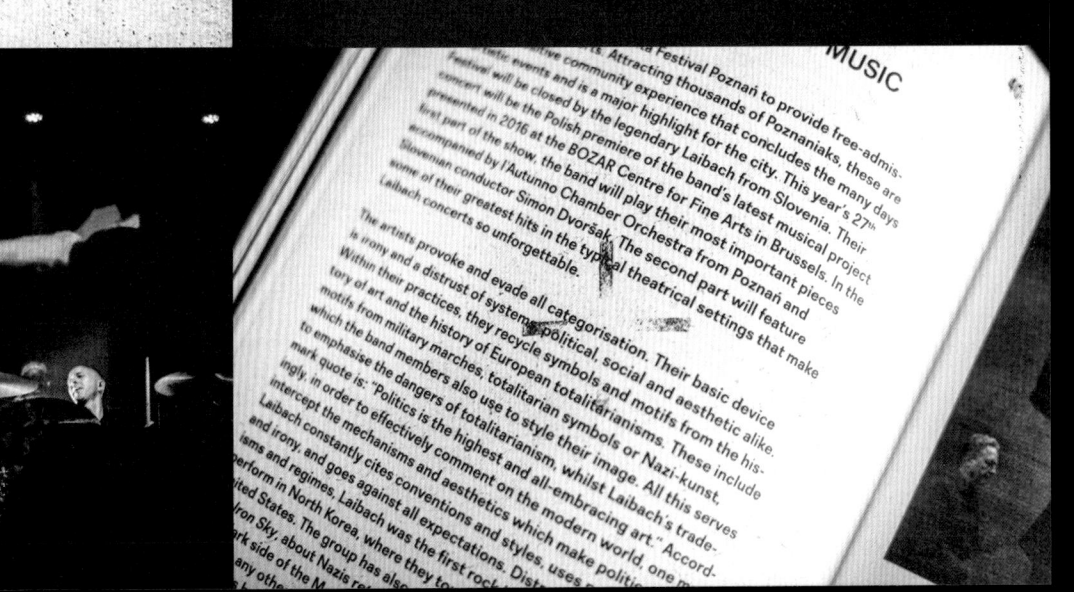

WEEK AGAINST BULLYING

AD, CD & D
Davy Denduyver

P
Daniil Lavrovski

2019

WAT WAT is a brand new youth platform issued by the Belgian government. Aimed at people aged 12 to 25, WAT WAT hopes to have the answers to a whole range of questions. WAT WAT did the official campaign for Belgium's national "Week Against Bullying".

For the poster campaign, the team decided to have a chat with the "influencées" spanning the campaign and talk about their personal experiences of bullying. Seeking a theme of honest engagement, the team photographed the models in sober outfits and superimposed quotes about bullying on their faces, reminding them not to be defined by those experiences.

Visually, the designer took cues from WAT WAT's funky shaped logo, and reinterpreted this as a straighter, more minimal shape, which then became a template for the photographs in order to empasize the candid, direct aspect of the campaign.

DESIGN PASAR 2019, SINGAPORE

AD & CD
Yah-Leng Yu

D
Dandy Hartono &
Sylvester Tan

2019

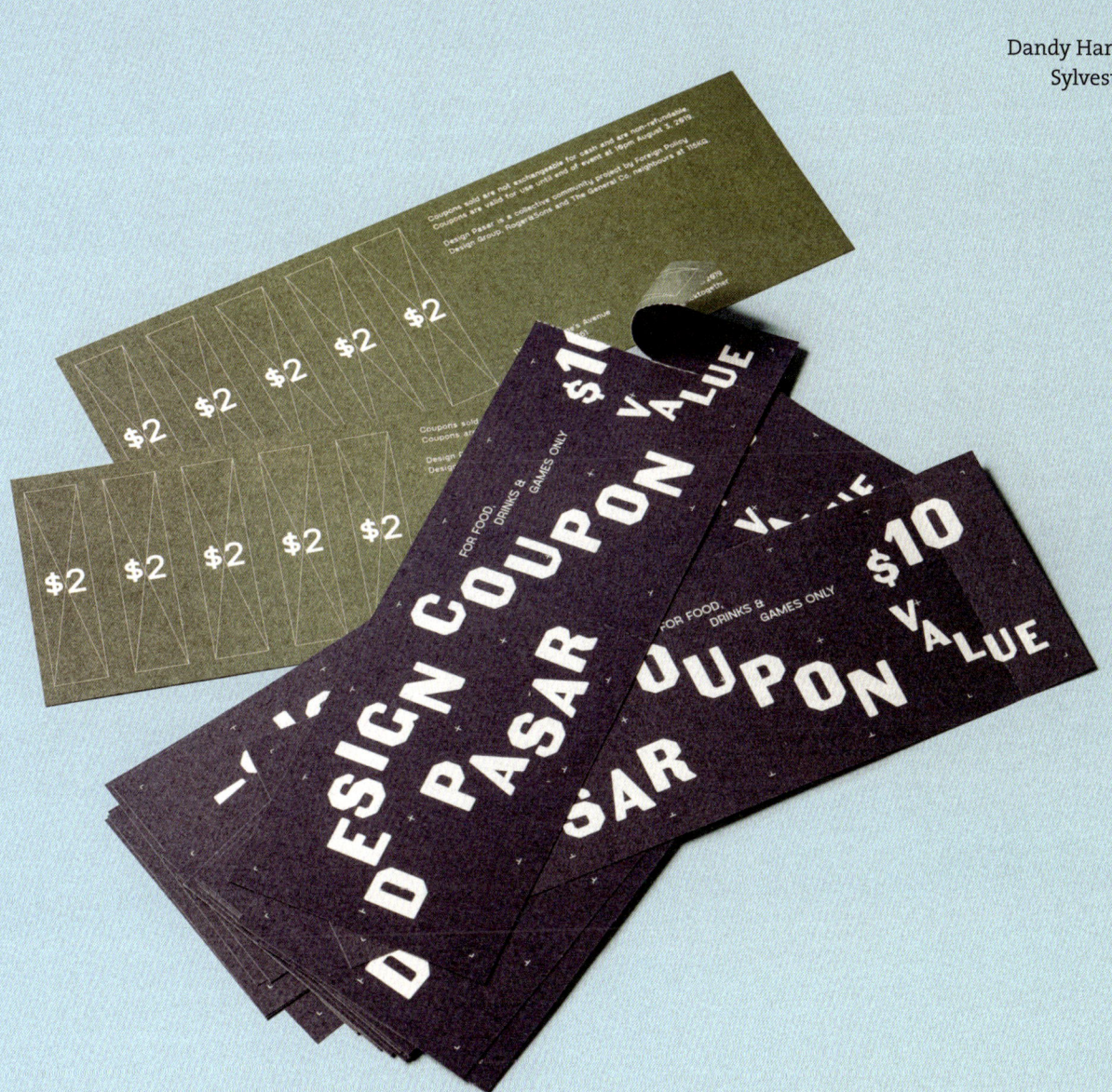

Design Pasar is about bringing design, craft and arts to the community and neighbors. It is inspired by and adapted from the traditional Pasar Malams (in Malayisan, Pasar Malam means "night market", which is often seen popping up in the neighborhoods in Singapore). Design Pasar hopes to elevate the neighborhood experience, allowing the general public to have greater access to affordable design, as well as locally-designed and locally-made goods, arts and music.

The theme for this edition of Design Pasar is "Sticking Together as a Community." It is also paying tribute to Singapore National Day and celebrating the progress Singapore has made in terms of developing a thriving and growing creative industry sector and vibrant communities. The brand visual identity takes its cue from the shapes of objects found in this neighborhood which is dominated by the hardware industry. These shapes are designed as stickers so that anyone can create and design their own tote bag or poster with these stickers—an analogy of the mission of Design Pasar—which is to get everyone to be creative and to participate in design.

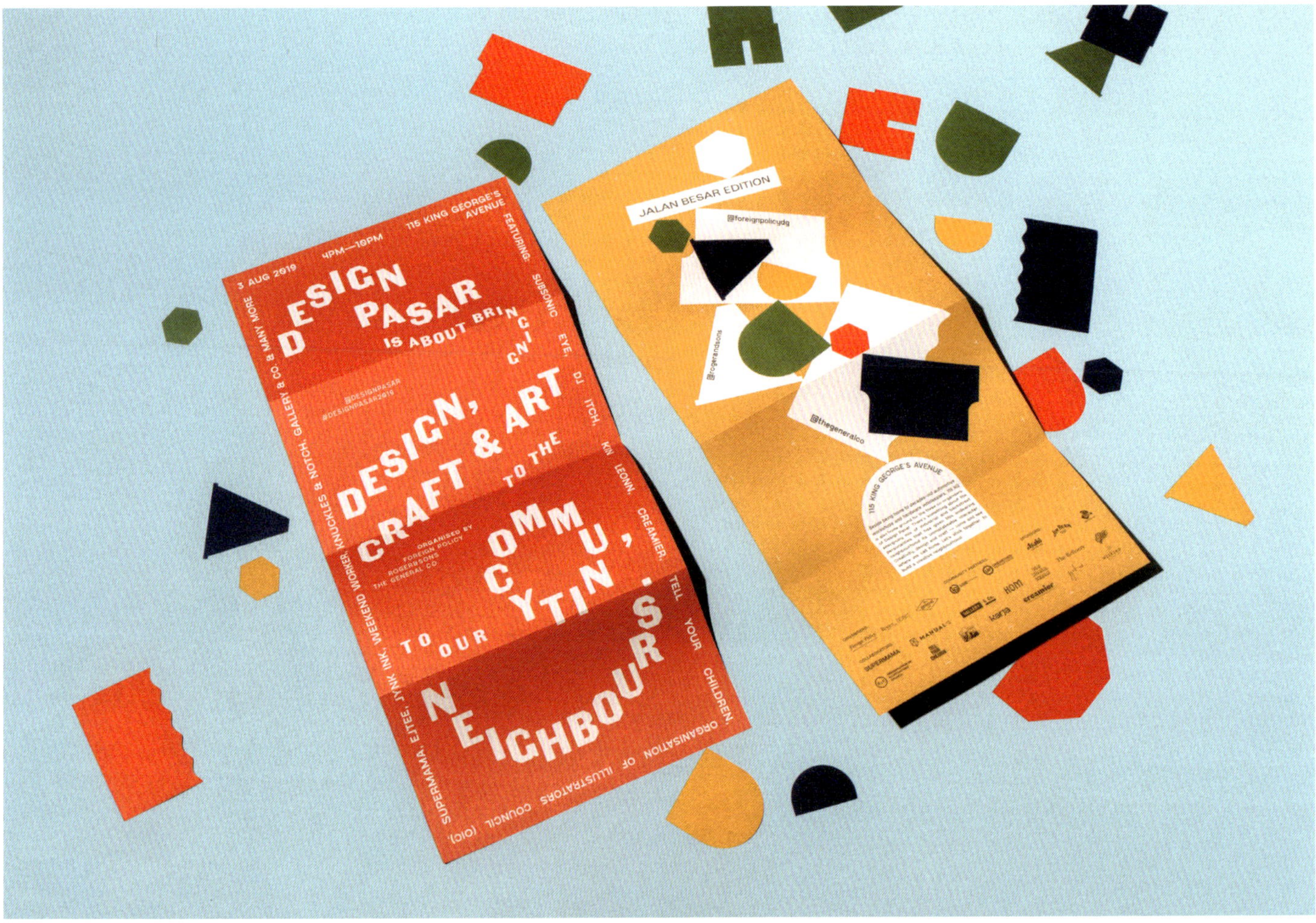
3 AUG 2019
4PM—10PM
115 KING GEORGE'S AVENUE
DESIGN PASAR IS ABOUT BRINGING
DESIGN, CRAFT & ART TO THE
COMMUNITY,
TO OUR NEIGHBOURS
ORGANISED BY FOREIGN POLICY ROGERSONS THE GENERAL CO
FEATURING: SUBSONIC EYE, DJ ITCH, KIN LEONN, CREAMIER, TELL YOUR CHILDREN, ORGANISATION OF ILLUSTRATORS COUNCIL (OIC), SUPERMAMA, EJTEE, JYNK INK, WEEKEND WORKER, KNUCKLES & NOTCH, GALLERY & CO. & MANY MORE
JALAN BESAR EDITION
@foreignpolicydg
@thegeneralco
115 KING GEORGE'S AVENUE

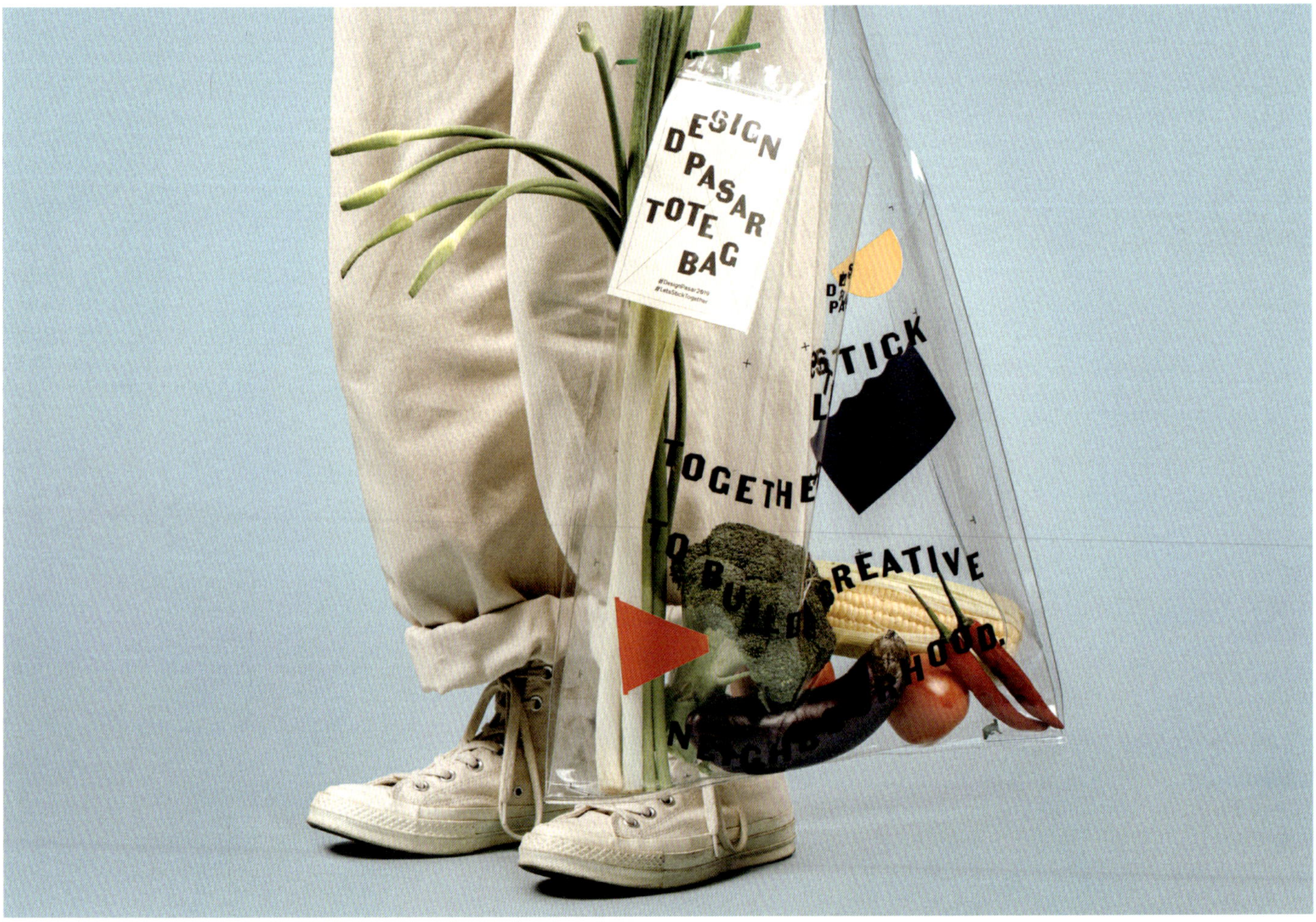
DESIGN PASAR TOTE BAG
TOGETHER
CREATIVE

BAD NEWS NEWSPAPER

AD & D
Raúl Kokott

CD
Bjoern Wolf & Fons Hickmann

P
diverse

DS
Fons Hickmann M23

2018

The designers feel they are inundated with real news, fake news, and bad news. The world is changing, but not always for the better. In keeping with this phenomenon, the second Wiesbaden Biennale for Performing Arts, which was held in the summer of 2018 in the Staatstheater Wiesbaden, has chosen "Bad News" as its theme. To promote the event, the designer created a newspaper that evoked the style of the tabloid press, with large, flashy fonts communicating the

SANTARCANGELO NON ESISTE

AD, CD, D & P
Alessandro Latela,
Sara Ceradini &
Cecilia Murgia

2019

Santarcangelo Festival is one of the most important Italian events dedicated to contemporary theater, dance and performing arts. Founded in 1971, the Festival comes to life in the city of Santarcangelo di Romagna in July.

Santarcangelo non esiste, which means "Santarcangelo does not exist", is the name of the project developed for the 50th anniversary of the Festival. The project aims to be a provocation, to reflect on the importance of the Festival in the city and on the value that this cultural institution has given to the territory over these years.

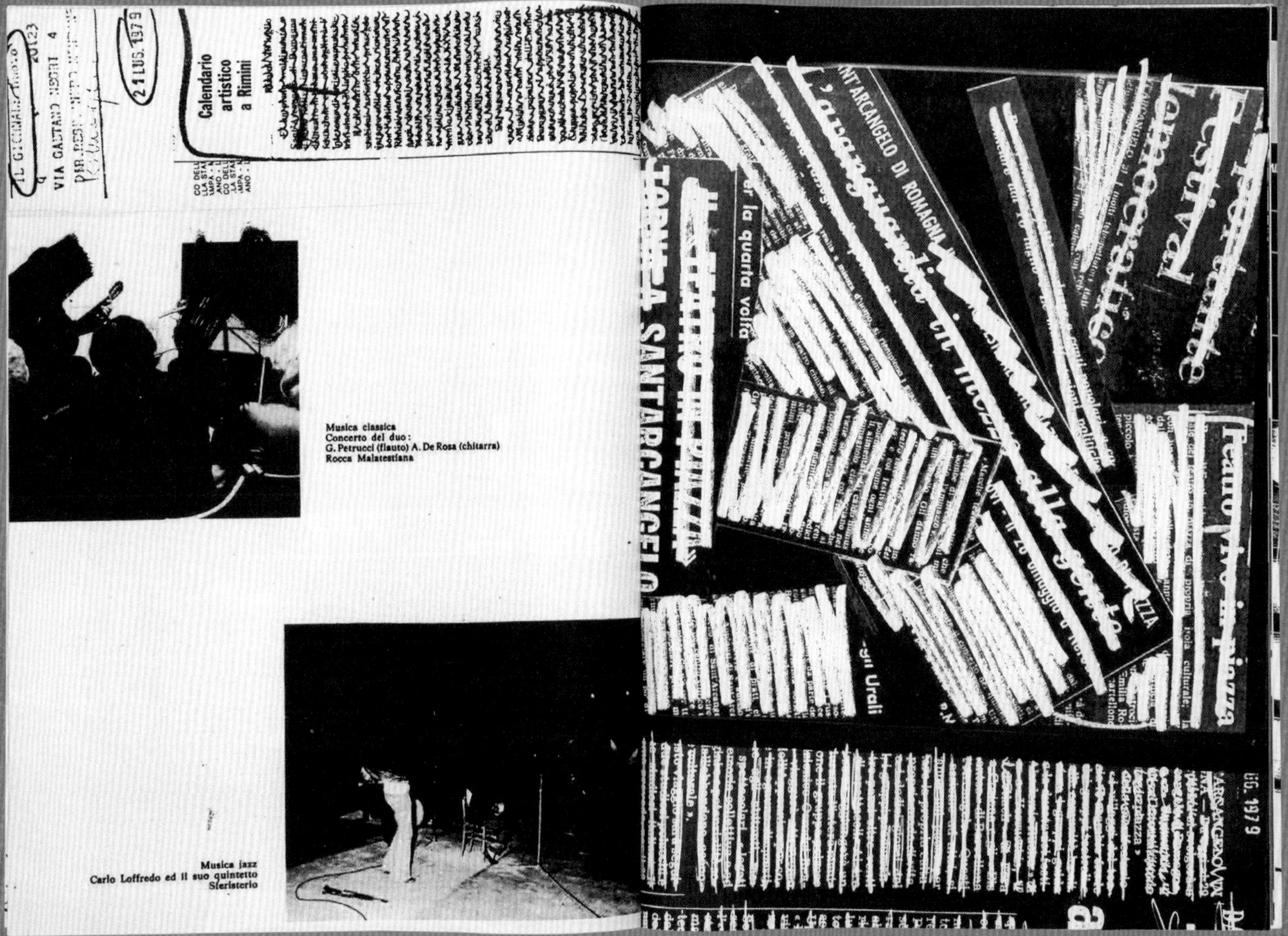
Calendario artistico a Rimini
21 LUG. 1979
Musica classica
Concerto del duo:
G. Petrucci (flauto) A. De Rosa (chitarra)
Rocca Malatestiana
Musica jazz
Carlo Loffredo ed il suo quintetto
Sferisterio
la quarta volta

Sciortino
martedì 13 luglio 2004
29

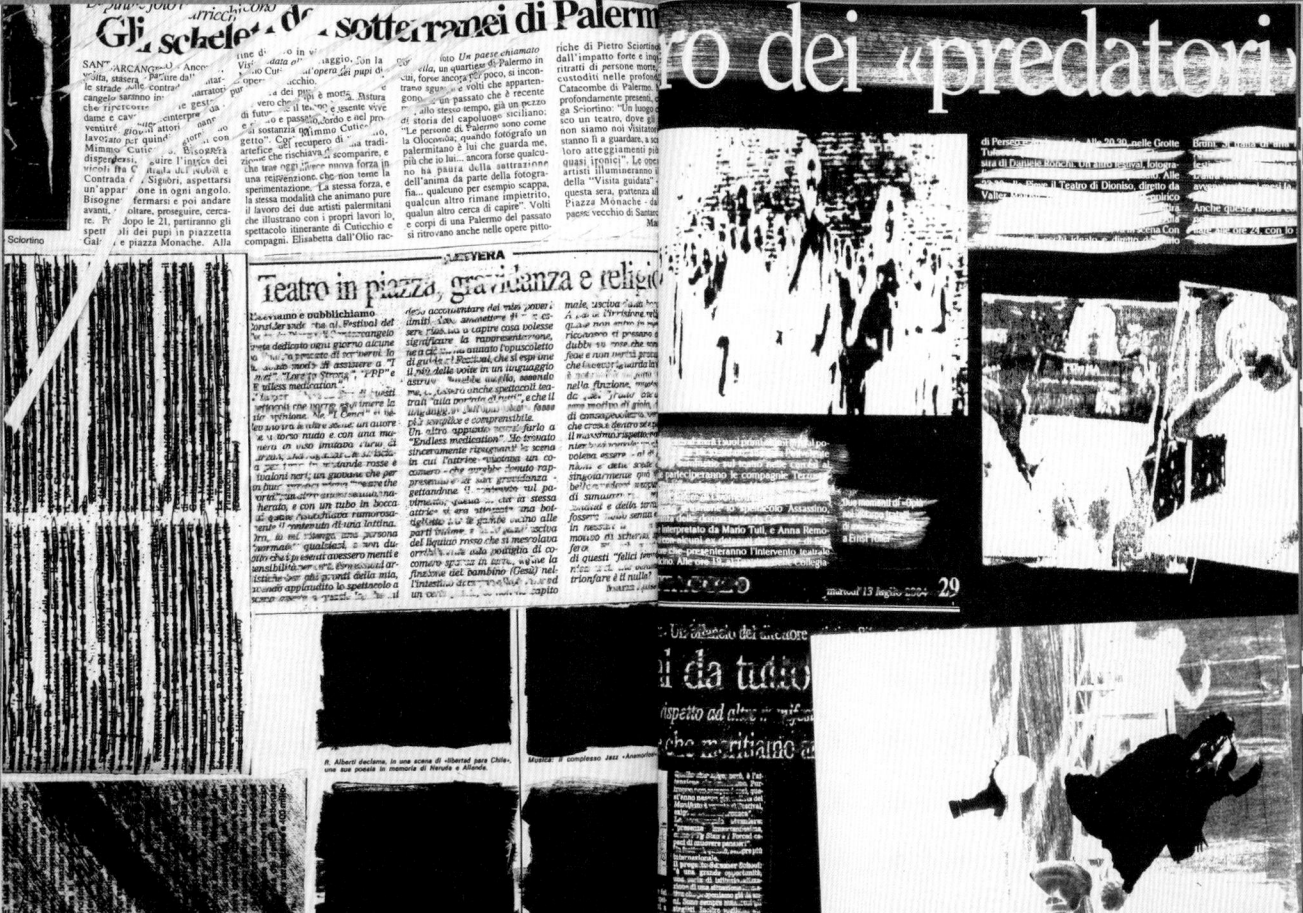

INTERMEDIA THEATER

D
Dokho Shin

2015

"Intermedia Theater" was held in 2015 at Nam June Paik Art Centre in Seoul and it aimed to look at his influence in a wide variety of media and disciplines. The designer found the diagram that Dick Higgins defined how interdisciplinary practice connects to each other, and adopted its form to make the identity of the exhibition.

D
Dokho Shin

2019

LIEDBasel has held this event since 2019 and its historical background is based on Lied (a German word meaning "Song", but at the same time it refers to a type of duet between a piano player and a singer). The slogan of the first event was "Die Gedanken sind frei" (meaning "Thought is free") and the designer's idea for the slogan was to evoke an air of ambiguity in audiences' interpretation.

VERS — ANYTHING GOES

D
Angello Torres

DS
The Whispering Sea

2019-2020

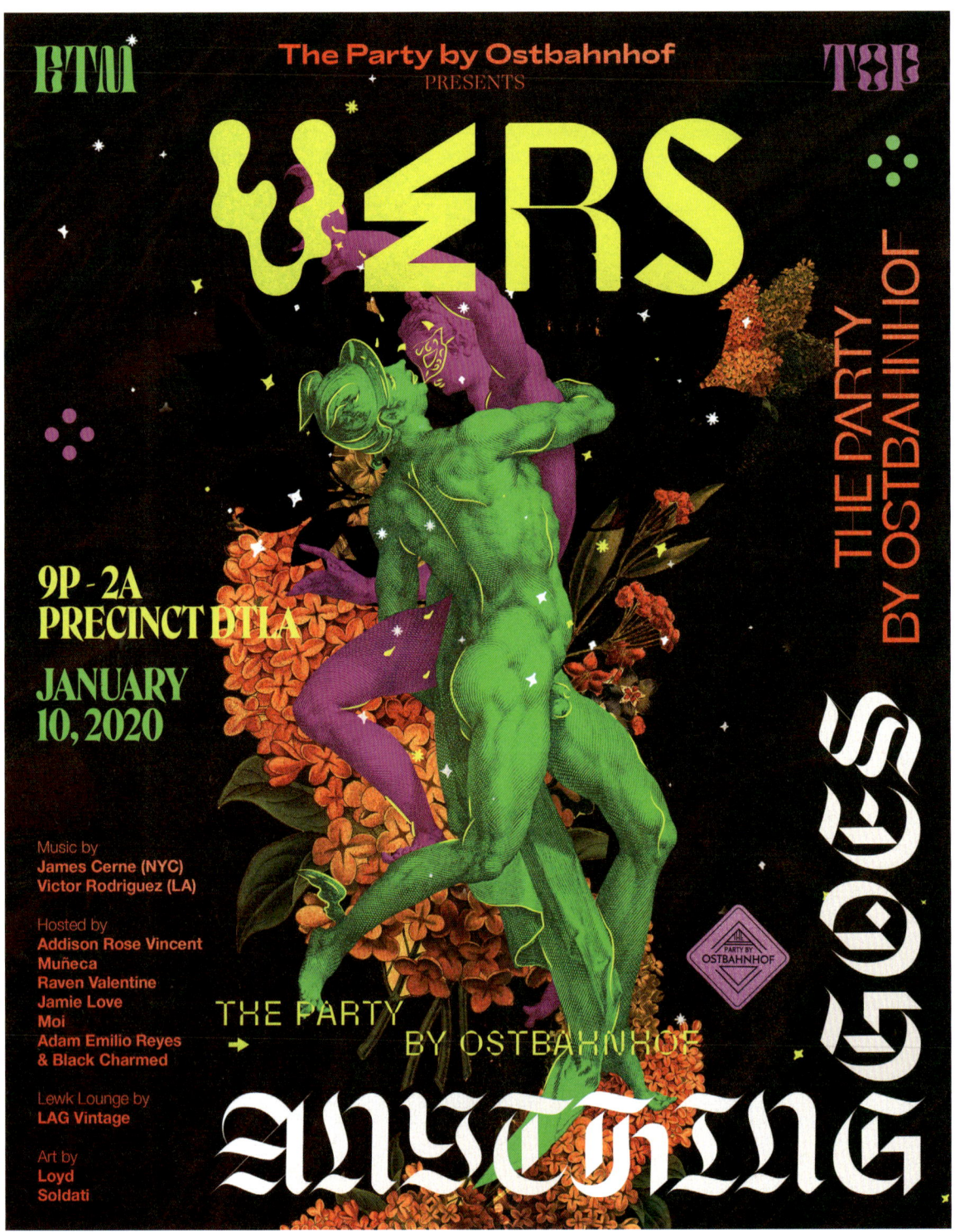

The Party by Ostbahnhof is a series of international events that seeks to bridge the gap between people through music, art, and political community, creating safer spaces where all LGBTQ+ people can delight in their lives. This design was created with the hope that everyone can have fun, feel free to express who they really are, and feel connected to the community.

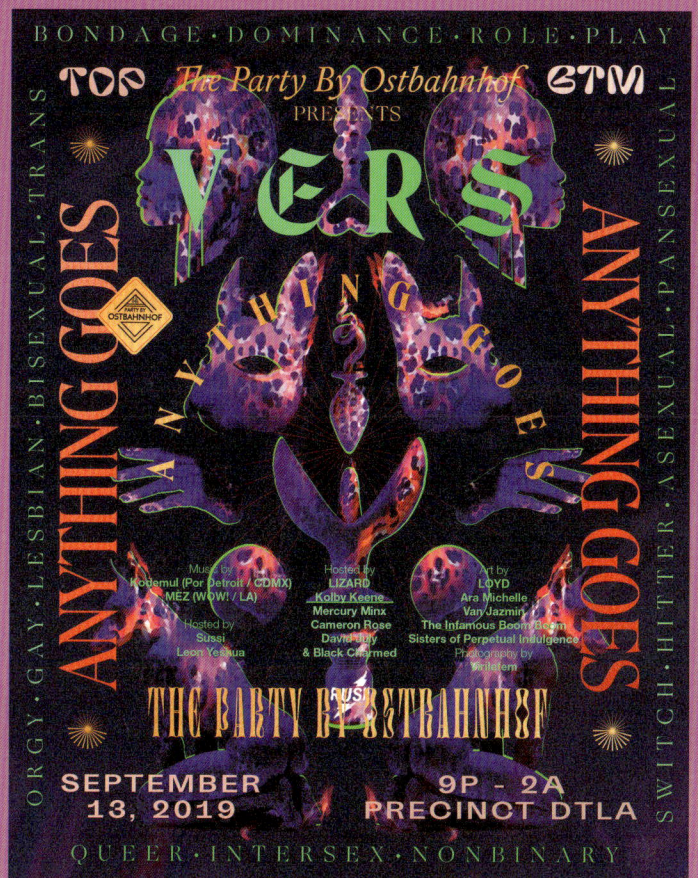
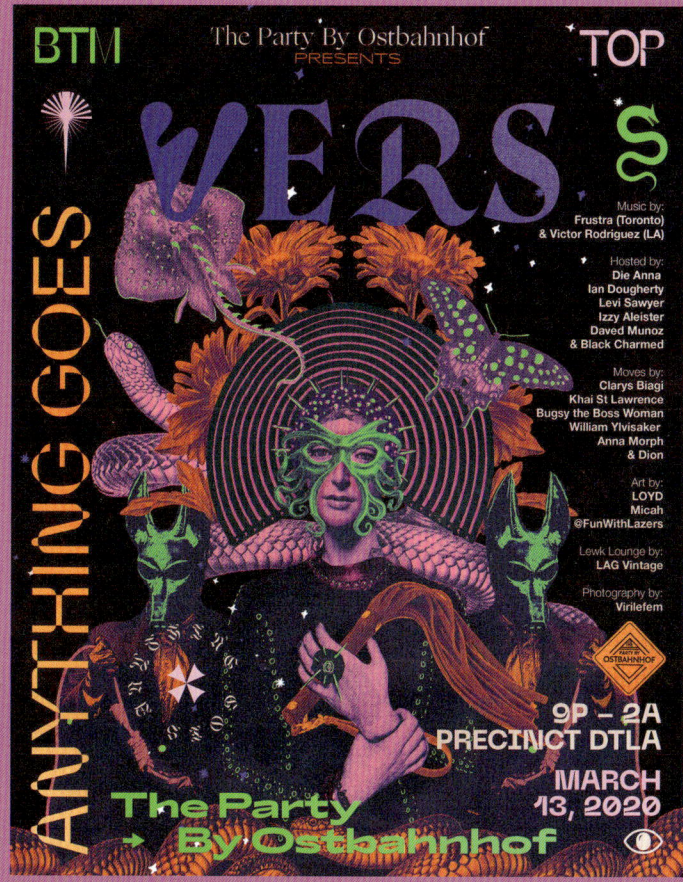
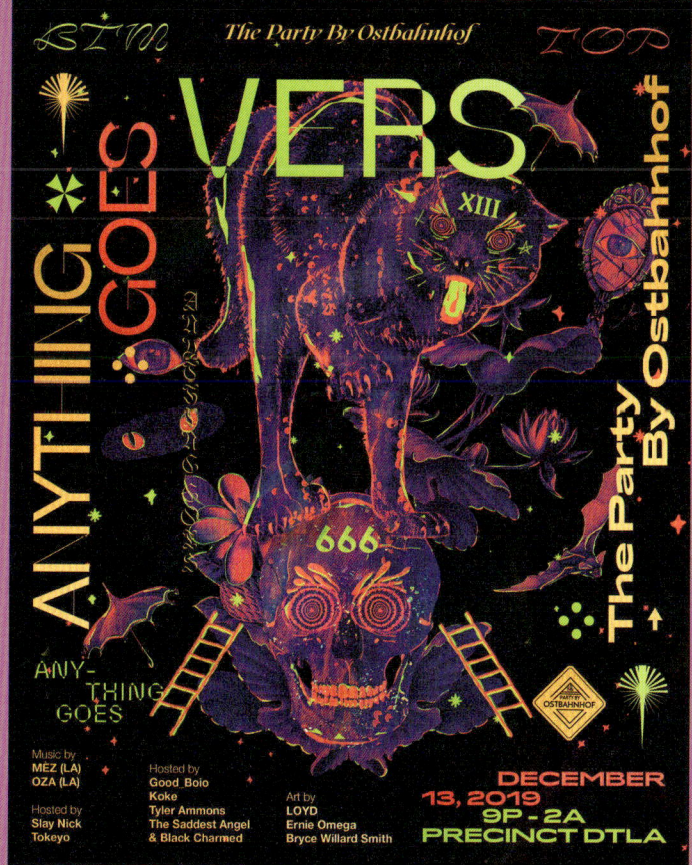
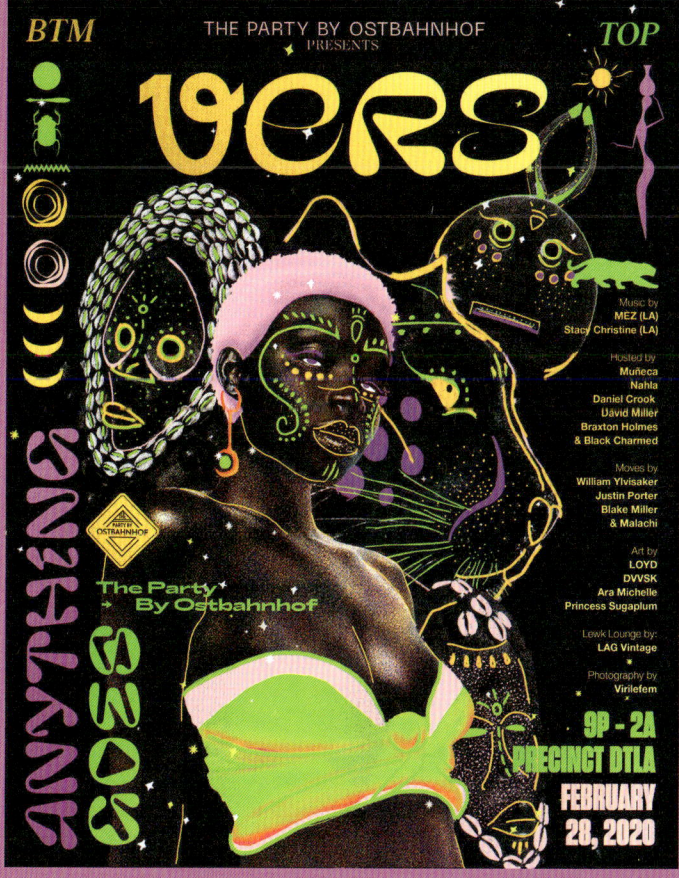

BLACK BELT — PROFESSIONAL SHOWCASE

B Branding

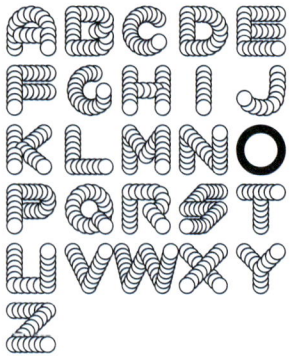
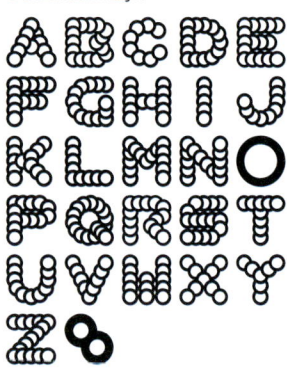
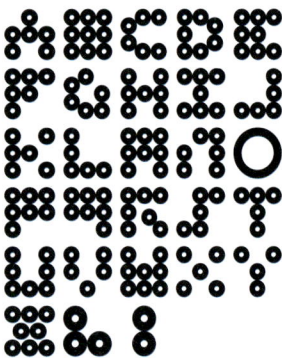

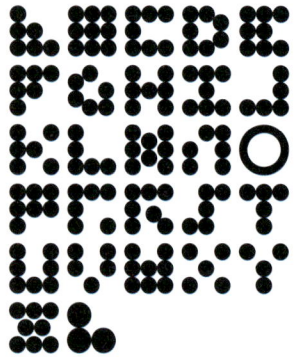

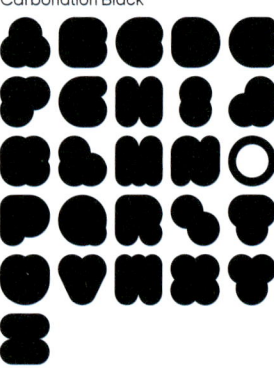

AD
Alice Mourou &
Gus Cheung

CD & P
Alice Mourou

D
Alan Wa Lun Wong

DS
.Oddity Studio

2019

THE CARBONATION

Carbonation is a new independent brand of fizzy cocktail mixers. The main concept is "Bubble language"—it makes use of basic bubble shapes to form a whimsical secret alphabet that captures a delightfully playful tone. They created a font family (with 7 styles) made of combinations of bubbles, where there is interplay between glyphs as well as Asian and Western typography. Glyphs form abbreviations that become key graphic elements and convey hidden messages: TW for Tonic Water and CBNT for Carbonation. The cultural background of this design articulates an opposition to the plain, uninspiring and oversaturated mass market in Hong Kong, and this sensibility allows Carbonation to gain a distinctive identity with a slight touch of mystery and the exclusivity implied in their hidden messages.

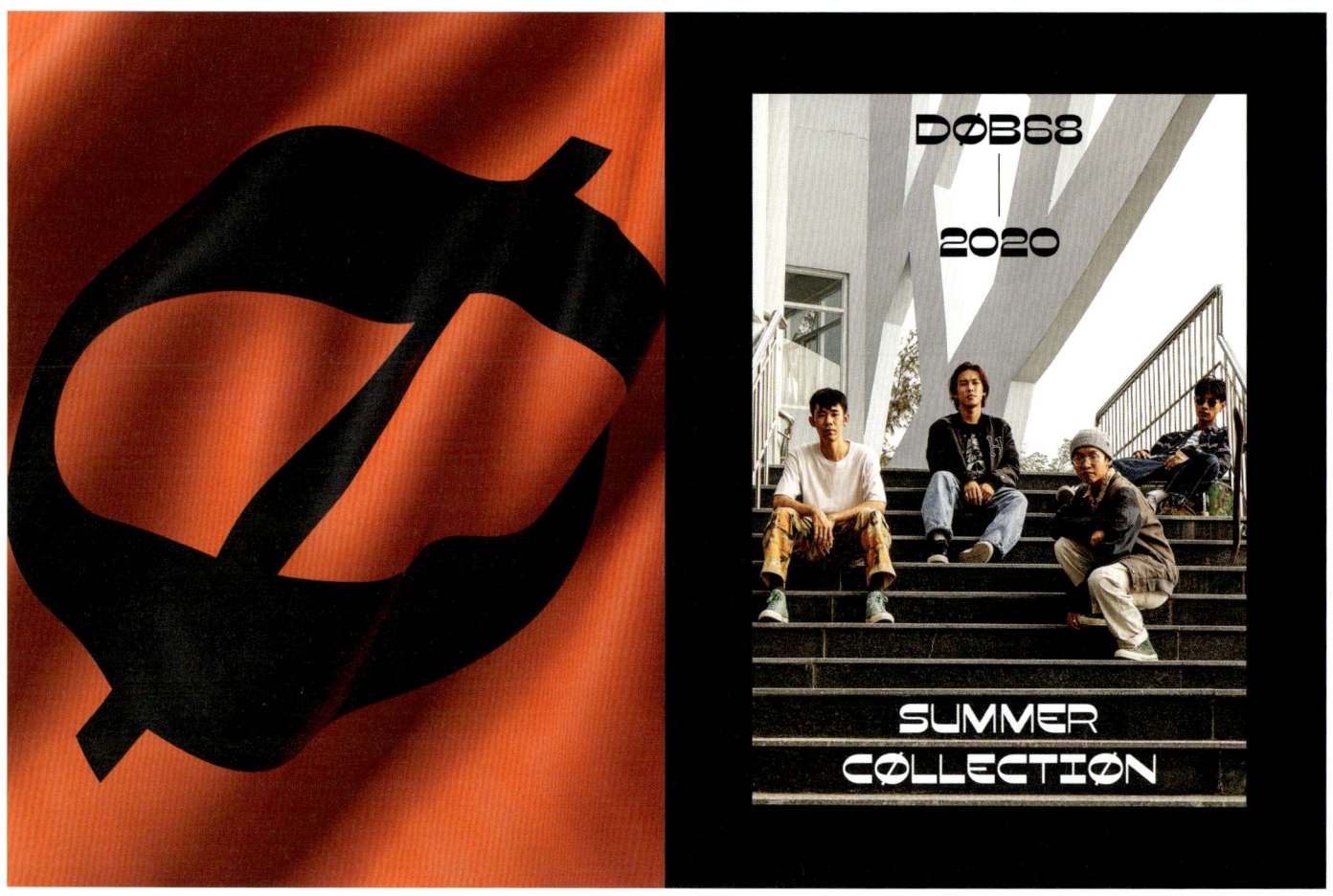

DOB DISPLAY — DOB68 BRAND TYPEFACE

D
Si Tran

P
Do Nam

2019

The team behind Dude on the Board 68 (DOB68) fashion brand were enthusiastic skateboarders. This passion inspired them to introduce handpicked vintage items that captured each skateboarder's personality, aesthetic sense and passion in pursuing what they love, leading to their own streetwear fashion brand for skaters was brought forth by 2019, and with it, there came the idea of DOB Display.

    True to its form, DOB Display is a manifestation of street youngsters constrained by limitations yet transforming into unique and passionate selves. With that in mind, the idea of a sans-serif typeface with inverted contrast was employed throughout the designs. Inspired by the shape of a skateboard, DOB Display contains rounded counters similar to a geometric shape, while the dramatic contrast between vertical and horizontal lines makes an immediate attention-grabbing visual impact.

THE LANGUAGE ØN THE STREETS

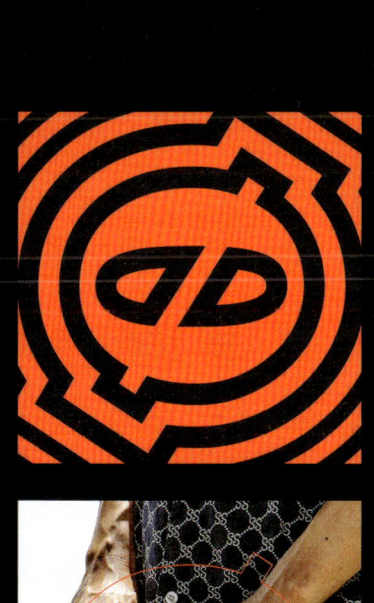

ADOBE CREATIVE CLOUD CAMPAIGN: EL TALENTO ESTÁ EN TODOS

AD
Paola Crespo & Nubia Navarro

CD
Juan Pablo Forero

D
Nubia Navarro Aka Nubikini

DS
Contenidos El Rey

2020

"El talento está en todos" is a very colorful campaign that these designers put together for Adobe Creative Cloud Latin America which focused on the concept of "Everyone has talent". They created a big visual universe focused on three types of thinking: individual, group and collective. These categories allowed them to develop characters, patterns and shapes to work together to re-emphasize the effectiveness of Adobe graphic tools for people in Latin American countries. Mailings, prints, T-shirts and social media posts were also utilized in this campaign.

DON'T FORGET TO HAVE FUN WHILE CREATING NEW THINGS
;)
Don't be afrait of making mistakes.
Take breaks
Find your flow
Always seek feedback
Click. Delete. Gone.

ATUALIZE SEUS PROJETOS COM A
Creative Cloud em 3, 2, 1 ...
Gradient
Type:
Draw: Points Lines
T

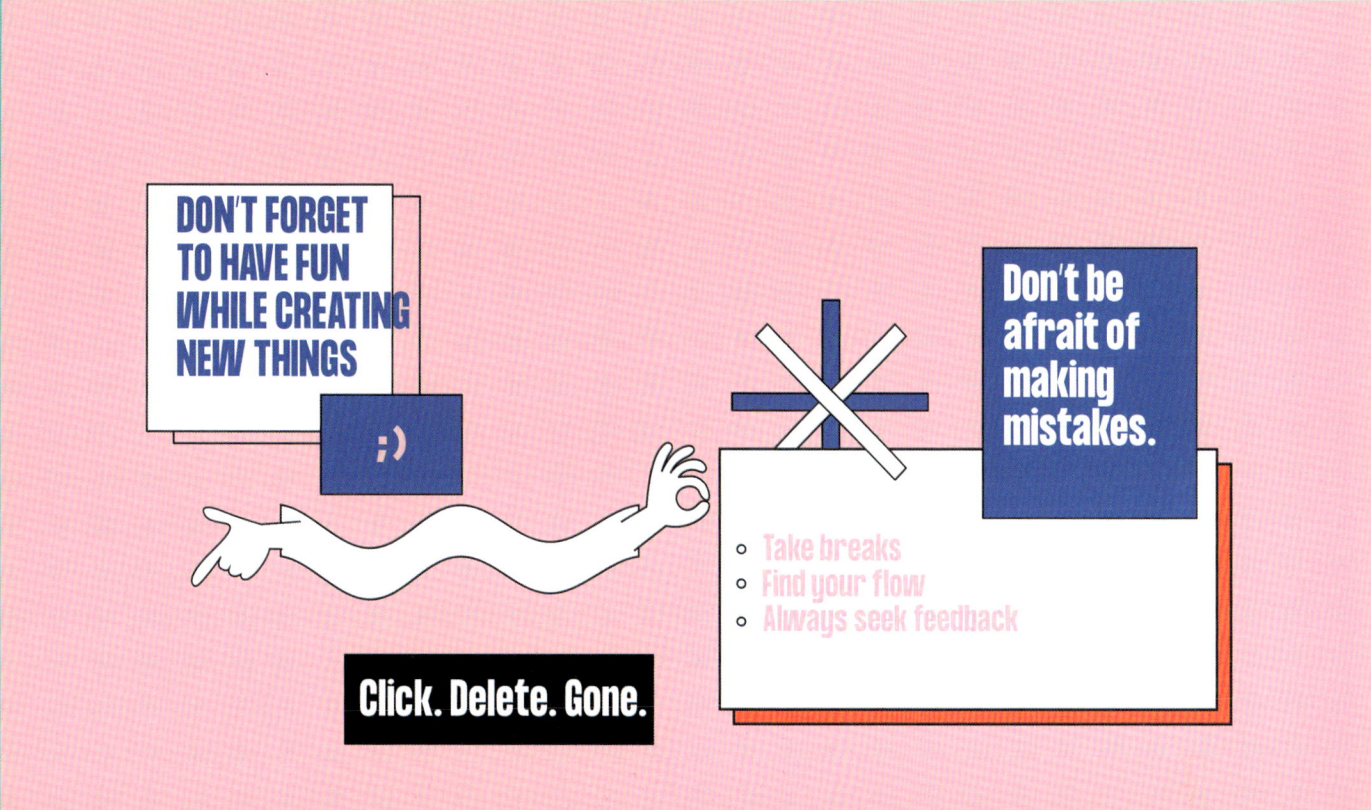

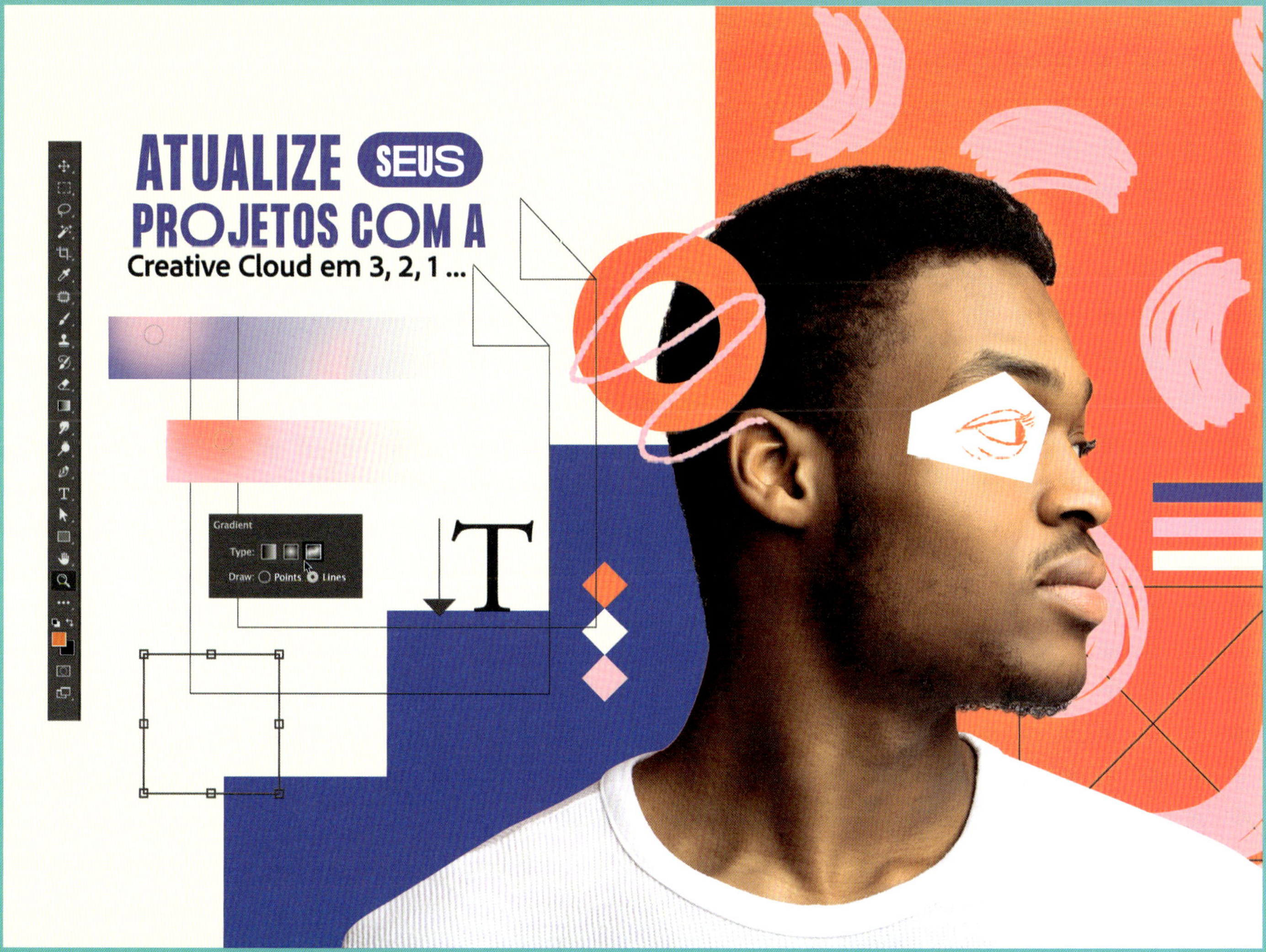

THE BELL JAR BOOK

CD, D & P
Aniko Mezo

2019

This is an illustration program of a typographic book, *The Bell Jar*, an autobiographical novel by Sylvia Plath which describes the protagonist's descent into mental illness. The designer created a variable font based on an existing typeface—Lora. The letters were created after a series of distortion experiments. The purpose of the project was to mirror in the typeface and the distortion of the letters, the descent of the protagonist into mental illness. The characters were distorted in the way that things seem visually deformed when viewed behind a glass, or a bell jar, so at the end of the book the letters become just visual marks, which are very hard to read or even almost unreadable—symbolizing the inexpressible feelings of the protagonist, who suffering from such extreme mental disorder and depression.

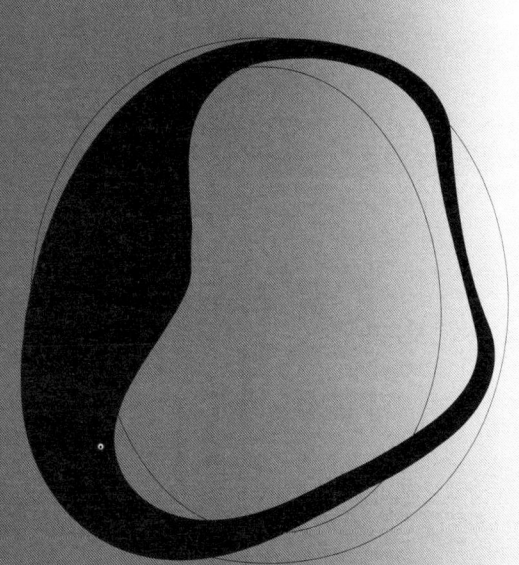

To the person
in the bell jar,
blank and stopped
as a dead baby,
the world itself
is a bad dream.

AD
Bora Shim

CD
Jehyung Kim

D
Chanju Yu & Borim Kim

DS
Studio Saworl

2020

EVERLAND HONEY PACKAGE

Everland, the biggest theme park brand of South Korea, collaborated with Ahn Sang-gyu Honey to launch a limited-edition merchandising that can remind people to value the sweet experience of having fun.

The title of the package—slang "ggul-jam" translates to "honey-fun", equating the extreme level of enjoyments to the sweetness of honey. The studio has designed four different graphics for different types of honey sachets in the package. And the designers used illustrations, appropriate colors and bold typography to portray the concept of fun packaging for honey products that links to the essence of the theme park.

THE TYPEFACE PROJECT

AD & CD
Jimmi Tuan

D
Si Tran, Nguyen X- Hoang & Alex Dang

P
084creative

DS
Bratus Agency

2020

The main purpose of Mặt chữ (meaning "typefaces") was to establish a packaging system for the coffee and cacao gifts of the Von Viet Project and Bratus. Inspired by the colonial culture and design in Vietnam, the Von Viet Project's designers took a journey back in time to explore and resurrect the most popular and outstanding typefaces in Saigon before 1975. They determined to make use of all typefaces by selecting random letters from each type and setting them on different faces of the box. That also explains the name of the project, Mặt Chữ. The final output was a multidimensional gallery of typefaces spread out across the packaging surface which tells its historic stories. It created an intriguing balance between the contemporary and the traditional in a packaging system. Also, the packaging can provide interactive fun for users if they pair boxes to form new typefaces.

YUMI ZOUMA

CD
Lorenzo Fanton

D
Lorenzo Fanton &
Margot Lévêque

2019-2020

The designer started to create this typeface called Romie in 2018, and it was until June 2019 that the design was finished and released. In November 2019, Lorenzo Fanton, saw one of the files opened on the designer's computer and asked the name of the typeface. Soon the collaboration started. Fanton was the Creative Director of Yumi Zouma. He asked the designer to draw a set of additional ligatures to build a visual identity.

TRUTH OR CONSEQUENCES

MODERN ART

AD & D
Valery Che

2019

Modern Art is a London-based gallery opened by Stuart Shave in 1998. Over 20 years the gallery has occupied six locations in East and Central London, and at present it is housed in a converted 5,000-square-feet pre-war factory building in the Clerkenwell area of Central London. Each year Modern Art participates in art fairs in Basel, Hong Kong, Miami, London, and New York.

GULLMUNN SPRITFABRIKK

CD
Erika Barbieri

D
Erika Barbieri & Henrik Olssøn

P
Anne Valeur

DS
Olssøn Barbieri

2019

The illustration technique used is pointillism, and 7 colors are utilized on the silkscreen design on the bottle. The decorated bottle invites the user to reuse the bottle as a carafe once the bottle is empty and the label is off. The main typographical label, printed on a subtle grey paper, is inspired by taxonomical documents, while the label at the bottom is gold hot-foiled.

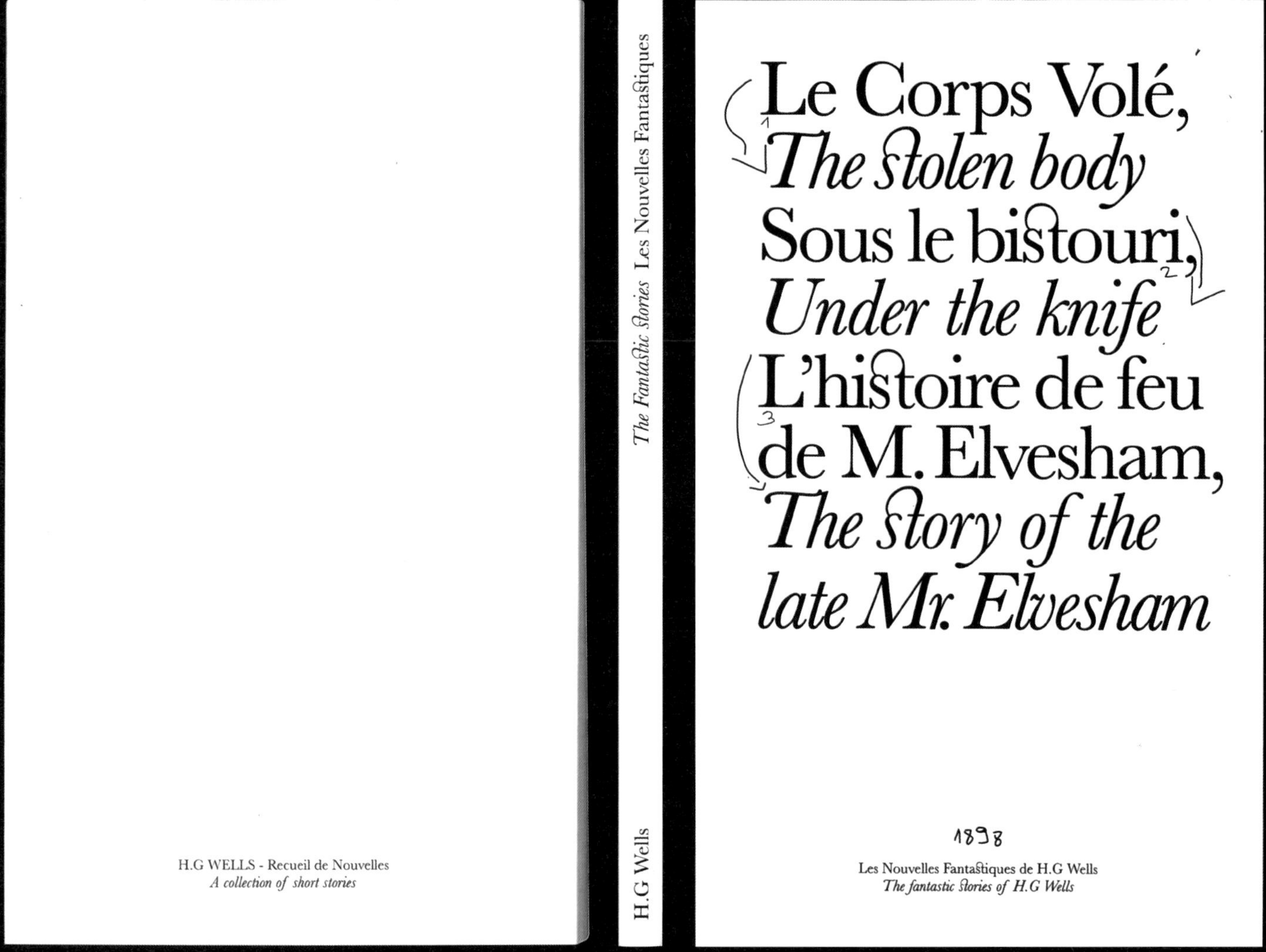

Le Corps Volé,
The stolen body
Sous le bistouri,
Under the knife
L'histoire de feu de M. Elvesham,
The story of the late Mr. Elvesham

1898

Les Nouvelles Fantastiques de H.G Wells
The fantastic stories of H.G Wells

H.G Wells

The Fantastic Stories Les Nouvelles Fantastiques

H.G WELLS - Recueil de Nouvelles
A collection of short stories

THE FANTASTIC STORIES OF H. G. WELLS

CD & D
Margot Lévêque

2019

This project aimed to create a bilingual literary novel (French and English) with three short stories from H. G. Wells who is known as the father of science fiction. The designer applied the usual process for this project—first the typography and the strict layout, then the dreamy and arty side of the process, where the designer had some freedom with iconography and colors, in order to create an aesthetic object.

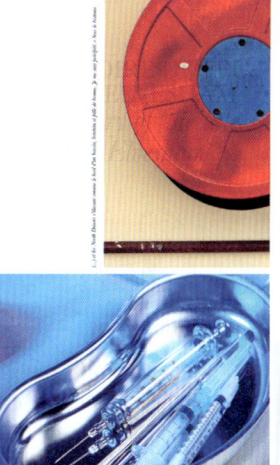

H.G. WELLS   L'HISTOIRE DE FEU DE M. ELVESHAM

301 semblait qu'un instant Regent street venait de me jouer ce tour ? Certain, néanmoins, que j'étais bien dans cette rue, je fus de nouveau troublé par de fantasques réminiscences qui affluèrent soudain. Il y a trente ans, pensai-je, c'est ici que je

305 me querellai avec mon frère. Mais aussitôt, j'éclatai de rire, au grand amusement d'un groupe de noctambules. Il y a trente ans je n'étais pas né, et je n'ai jamais pu me vanter d'avoir un frère. Cette mixture que j'avais bue était certainement de la folie liquide car un regret poignant de ce frère perdu

310 s'obstinait à m'étreindre. Au long de Portland Road, cette aberration prit une autre forme. Je me souvins de boutiques qui n'existaient pas, et je comparai la rue avec ce qu'elle était autrefois. Il n'y avait rien d'étonnant à ce qu'après un plantureux dîner, copieusement arrosé, mes pensées fussent

315 quelque peu désordonnées, mais j'étais fort perplexe à cause de ces réminiscences fantastiques, si curieusement précises, qui envahissaient mon esprit, et j'étais interloqué non seulement des souvenirs qui se présentaient, mais surtout de ceux qui m'échappaient. Je m'arrêtai devant la vitrine d'un

320 naturaliste, me mettant le cerveau à la torture pour retrouver ce qui pouvait bien m'intéresser là. Un omnibus passa avec un tintamarre qui ressemblait de façon extraordinaire au roulement d'un train.
   — Ah ! j'y suis ! fis-je à la fin. Je dois venir chercher ici,

325 demain, trois grenouilles à disséquer. N'est-ce pas curieux que j'aie oublié ? Quand j'étais enfant, on me donna pour jouet un kaléidoscope.
   Les dessins se chassaient les uns les autres et se superposaient : c'est de la même manière que cette série de sensations nouvelles s'efforçait de se substituer à celles de mon ordinaire

330 individu. Toujours perplexe et un peu effrayé, je gagnai Tottenham Court Road par Euston Road, sans remarquer quel chemin je prenais, car, d'habitude, je coupais à travers le réseau de petites rues environnantes. En tournant dans University street, je constatai que j'avais oublié le numéro

335 de ma maison. Il me fallut un violent effort de mémoire pour être certain que c'était le 11, et, même alors, j'eus l'impression qu'un inconnu me l'avait soufflé. J'essayai de raffermir mes idées en évoquant les incidents du dîner, et, quoi que je fisse, il me fut impossible de me rappeler les traits

340 de mon hôte. Je ne le voyais qu'en contours vagues, comme on s'aperçoit dans une vitre. À sa place, je distinguais, devant une table, une image de moi-même, rouge, loquace et les yeux brillants. Ça devient insupportable. Il faut que je prenne cette autre poudre, pensai-je. Je cherchais mon chandelier

345 et les allumettes du côté du vestibule où il n'y avait aucun meuble, et je ne savais plus à quel étage je demeurais. Je suis ivre, c'est certain, marmottai-je, et je trébuchai maladroi-

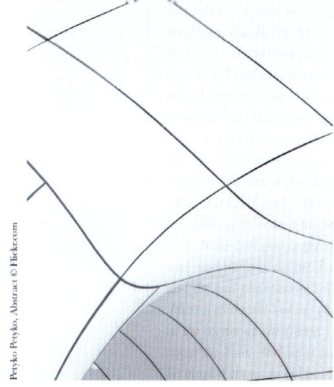

STUDIO LORE

AD & D
Ivo Pallucchini &
Jose Bessega

CD
James Yeats Smith

P
Bart Oomes

DS
AMATEUR(DOT)ROCKS

2019

Studio Lore is a creative studio in Amsterdam. The designers created a conceptual brand identity based on a contemporary and bold aesthetics.

The designers used the International Phonetic Alphabet to form the foundation of this typographic identity. They worked with Sharp Type to develop a bespoke 53 characters phonetic alphabet applied across the system, giving Studio Lore a distinct visual profile and voice in the creative industry.

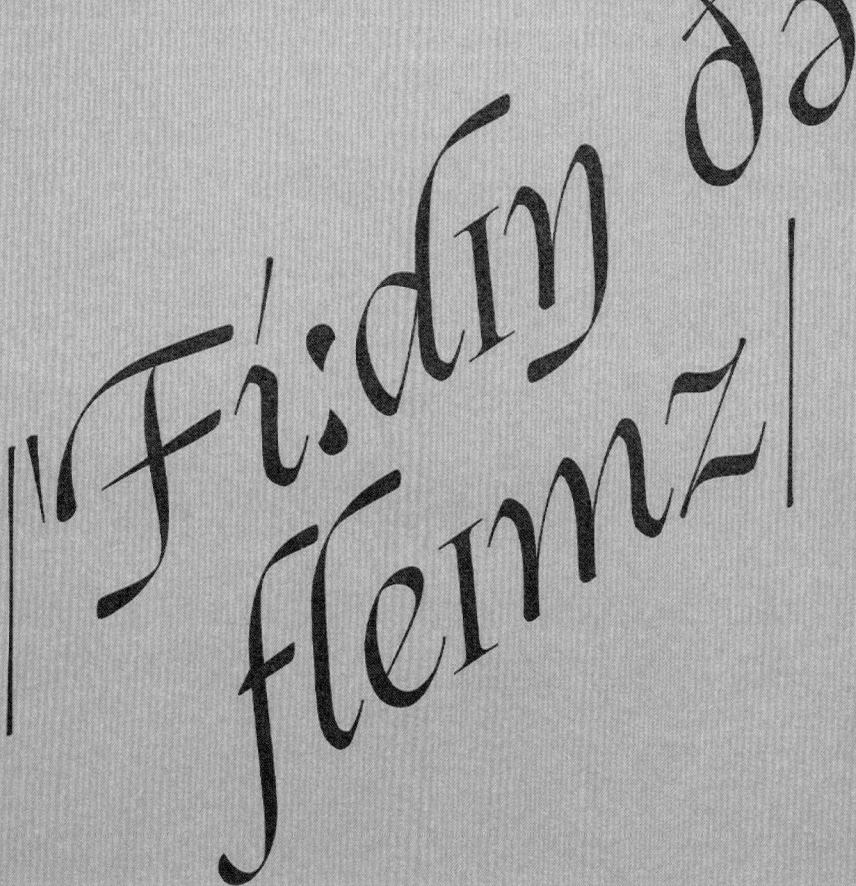

SUPERAR

Kostenlose Musikförderung für jedes Kind.

superar.eu

SUPERKINDER, SUPERAR.

AD & D
Johanna Jaksch

CD
Volkmar Weiss

P
Jork Weisman

DS
moodley design group

2020

The non-profit association Superar was founded in 2009 in order to change society in a positive way through music. The aim is to provide access to music education free of charge for children who otherwise would not have access at all.

Portraits that are full of expression, strength and emotion form the centerpiece of the corporate design. The concept of using the text to spell out the names of the participating children is not only an expression of solidarity with the children, but also highlights the importance of participation in this association. The specially created super-smiley face and the strong use of typography paired with the strikingly minimalist look, carry the message of Superar into the world—Here we make music, not distinctions.

IN MEMORY OF HAECHUL SHIN 1968-2014

D
Dokho Shin

2018

Haechul Shin was an influential singer in South Korea and passed away in 2014. This book has been released to commemorate his life and work. The designer aimed to design a strong cover as a tombstone with his respect.

D
Dokho Shin

2017

RECONSTRUCTION OF TRAJECTORY

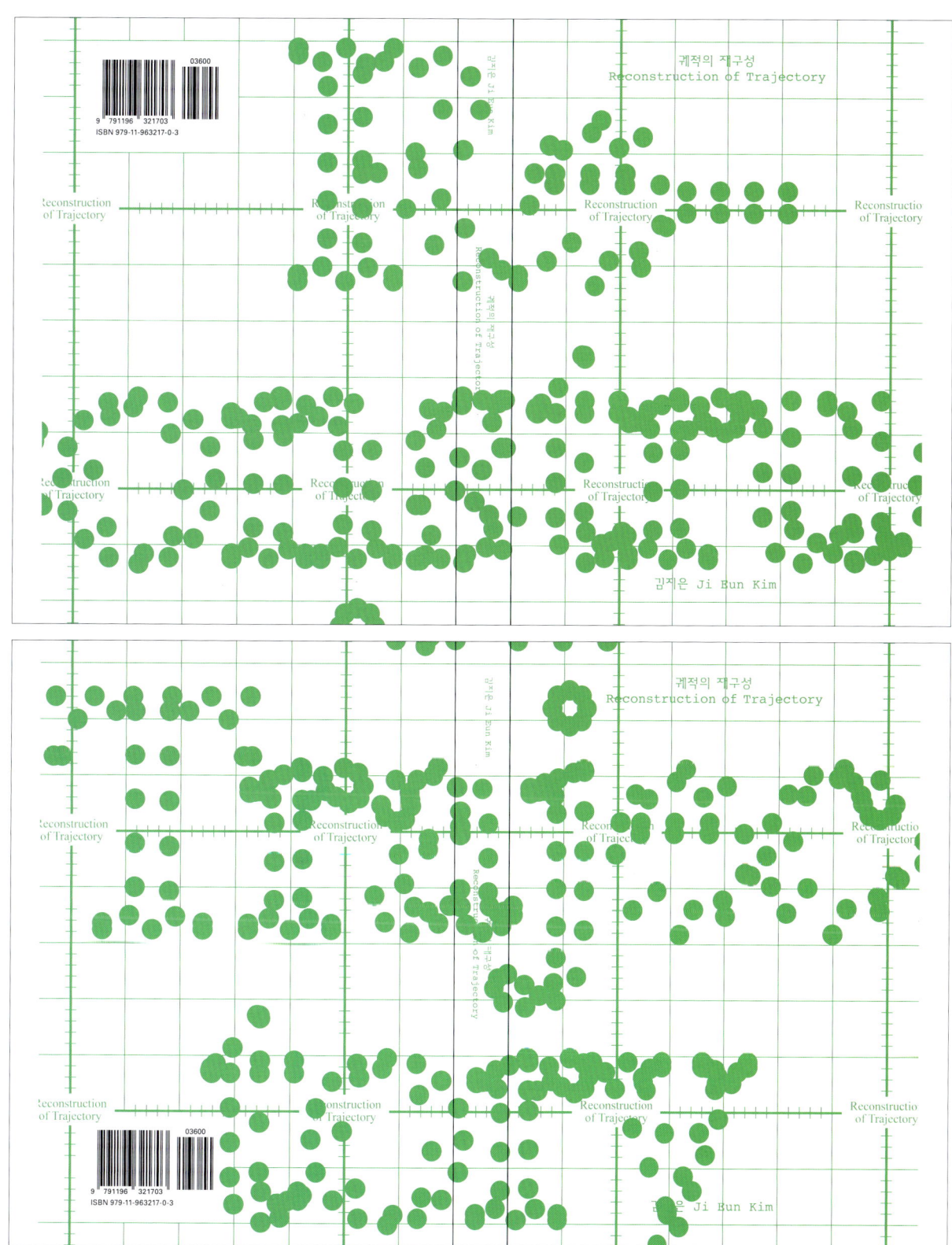

Jieun Kim is an artist who has had residencies in many countries and this book is a kind of report summarizing her artistic footprint over 10 years. Influenced by the word "trajectory", the designer made the typography an image that seems to trace its own shape.

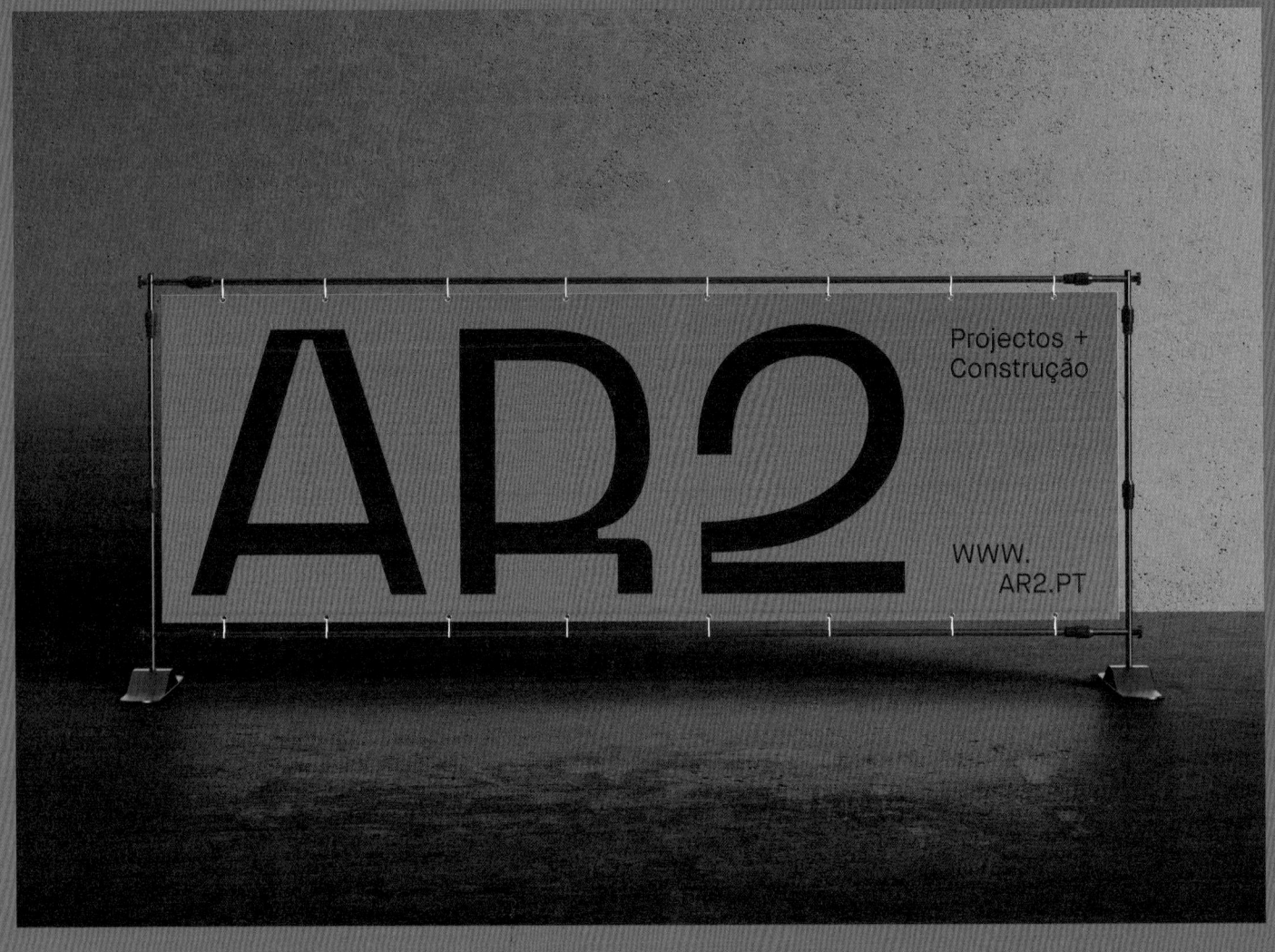

AR2 PROJECTOS + CONSTRUÇÃO

CD & D
Bruno Soares &
Eduardo Rodrigues

DS
Another Collective

2019

In this project, the designers strived for a modern approach, oriented towards a niche market with a pronounced attention to detail that values exclusivity above all. Thus, inspiration arises from the artistic currents of the first half of the 20th Century, using the past as a parallel to the work developed by AR2—a modernity that takes inspiration from what was done in the past.

This dichotomy is represented not only in the type, but also in the modern use of color, which contrasts with the brand, in order to take audiences to another time. It is an aesthetic duality that they seek to highlight across the whole identity. The fonts used in this project were Neue Machina for the logo and Maison Neue Book for the text.

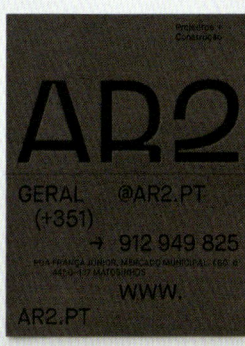

LABEL CONCEPT STORE

CD
Tuan Le

D
Ngoc Vo, Hung Le (Reo),
Uyen Dong & Thao Tran

P
Phong Chac & Thuy Truc

DS
The Lab Saigon

2017

Label Concept Store is a playground for creative experimentation. The designers' branding system allows them to put a label on any products, and their interior design allows for reinterpretation of the space.

The designers chose glossy color materials, printed in oversized formats to represent the kaleidoscope of creatives in Saigon. People don't have to look far beyond the neon lit streets to find a creative toiling away on something interesting, from ceramics, graphics, and furniture, to augmented reality AR.

C Concept

BLACK BELT—PROFESSIONAL SHOWCASE

WHISPER COLLECTION

D
Angello Torres

DS
The Whispering Sea

2019-2020

A series of fictional posters on film and music themes.

ERKIN FONT

AD, CD & D
Murathan Biliktü

DS
Cognoscenti Studio

2020

The designer wanted to create something that would look eccentric and could fit perfectly on the album cover of Erkin Koray (the legendary Anatolian rock artist), but could still be used on modern designs. This typeface has been the designer's signature font since its release, and it is definitely carrying the spirit of Erkin Koray.

AD
Yan Wang

2020

BLACK BELT—PROFESSIONAL SHOWCASE

CUPID BLUE

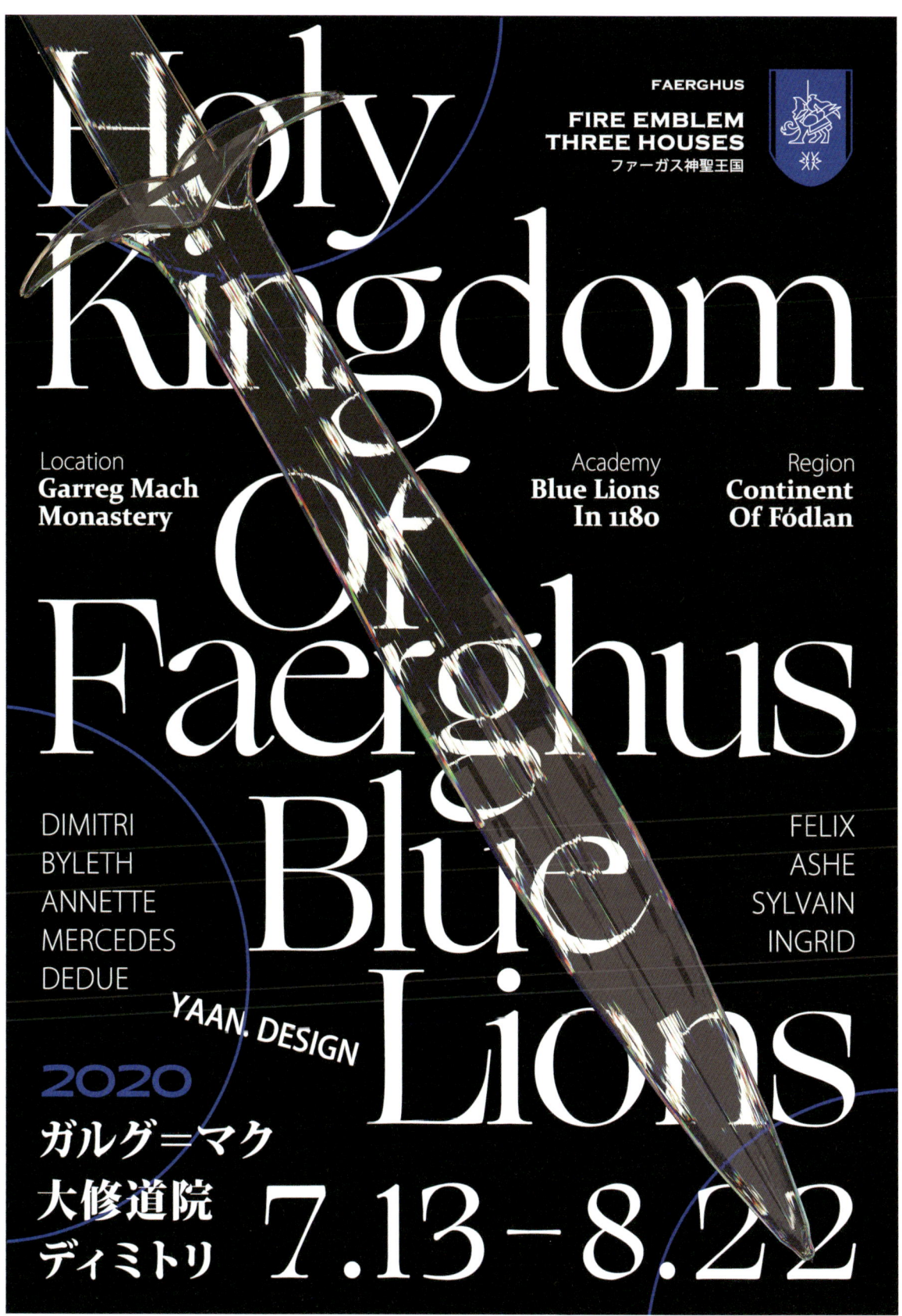

This series of posters was the result after the designer exploring the possibilities of combining type design, layout and illustration. At the same time, she tried to strike a balance between "acid design" and traditional layout, thus using some exaggerated elements while retaining the overall sense of order and logic.

THE OISEAUX

D
Angello Torres

DS
The Whispering Sea

2019-2020

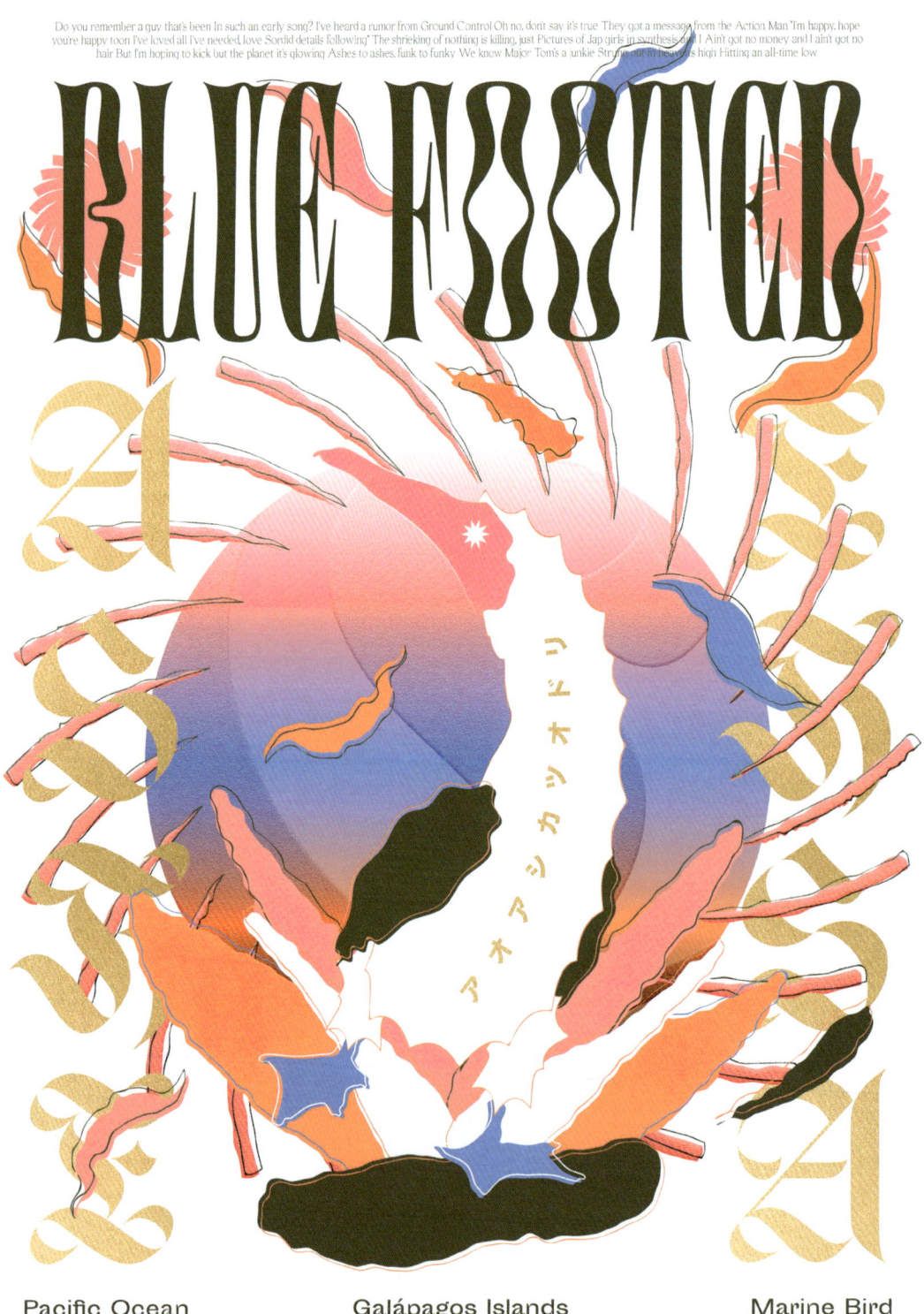

Pacific Ocean — Galápagos Islands — Marine Bird

A series of posters about Rain Poems and Botany.

SIEMPRE QUE ME PUEDA DIBUJAR
SOBRE UN NARANJA IMPAR,
COMO UN SUEÑO QUE NO TIENE DUEÑO,
VOY TEJIENDO TRES INTENTOS DE COLOR.
SÓLO SOY UN BICHO DE CRISTAL,
SÓLO SOY DE LUZ PIRAMIDAL.
QUE SE PIERDE CUANDO NO SE MUEVE
Y SE SIENTE UN PEZ LUNA EN TU INTERIOR.
CUANDO UN DÍA SIN SOL ENTRE EN TU HABITACIÓN.
SÓLO SOY DE CERA Y DE PAPEL.
SÓLO SOY LO QUE NO QUIERO SER.
Y NO ENTIENDO CÓMO ES QUE EL TIEMPO
VA TEJIENDO MIS INTENTOS DE COLOR.
CUANDO UN DÍA SIN SOL ENTRE EN TU HABITACIÓN.

I N T E N T O S   D E

BLACK BELT — PROFESSIONAL SHOWCASE

FLOWERS

AD, CD & D
Carmen Nacher Rodriguez

2020

Roses are Red, Violets are Blue, I'm a Bird of Paradise, Who are You?

Flowers is a personal project consisting of 3 posters. Each poster shows a picture of a flower together with text. The aim was to create a personalized design and lettering that would mirror not only the physical shape but also the aesthetics of the flower in the picture.

RANDOM POSTER COLLECTION

AD, CD & D
Marcello Raffo

2020

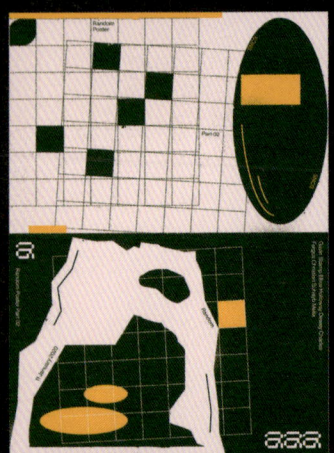

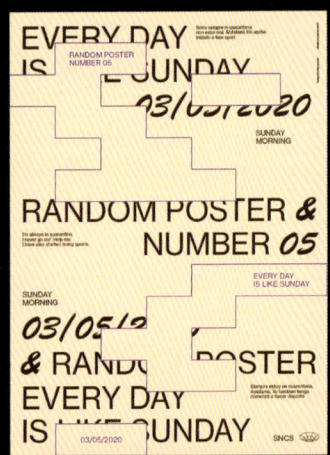

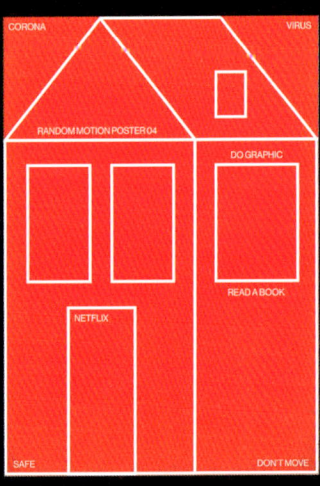
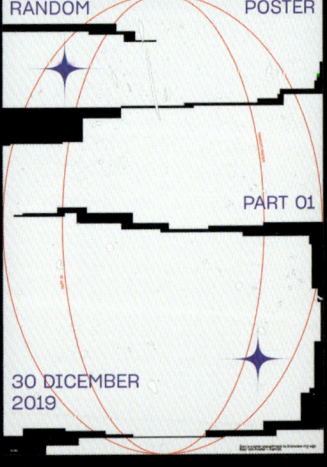

The project was designed during the last few months of 2020 to improve designer's graphic skills and experiment with new visual forms of expression. The designer tried to settle on a personal style, characterized by a large use of colors and flat monochrome shapes. The typography is a relevant and recurrent element inside all the posters. It facilitates completeness and balance in the posters in order to transform a simple frame of abstract shapes into an artifact. Some of those typefaces are created by the designer. The posters took inspiration from the digital world, not only by the use of flat colors, but also from the pixel-shaped elements and the use of grids.

D
Taras Rusych
2019

KINETIC TYPE EXPLORATIONS

This is the designer's first personal project in motion deisgn. The goal was to emake 10 "poster-like" animations with typography animators, to learn tricks of After Effects, to try some experiments with 3D layers and to enhance the designer's vision of minimalistic animations.

KUNSTHALLE ERFURT

CD & D
Ondine Pannet

DS
Bureau Est

2018-2020

US POSTCARDS

AD, CD & D
Steven Wilson

DS
Steven Wilson Studio

D
Miyu Shirotsuka

DS
Wieden + Kennedy

2017

MIRROR

This poster is inspired by a quote by Lady Bird Johnson: "The environment is not only a mirror of ourselves, but a focusing lens on what we can become." The designer loves this quote because it reminds people of the parallels between human activity and the health of the environment through a positive but actionable message. It taught the designer that the simple intention to actively care for the Earth—through small but meaningful actions—can enhance not only the environment but also the person.

UPCYCLED WITH LOVE

AD & D
Maria Dierkes & Florian Loi

CD
Henning Otto & Elisabeth Plass

DS
EIGA Design

2018

At the end of 2018, the designers produced an example of sustainable design that rethought the concept of sustainability in a completely different way by using plastic waste. This resulted in a personalized greeting card made of things that appear to no longer have a purpose.

They cut out transparent letters from used plastic bags. The font was designed specifically for the project. Combinations of the customers' initials were repeatedly hand printed onto the cards, which were recycled from straw. For the final step, the copy text and seal were stamped on.

AD, CD & D
UV-Zhu

2020

MIX AND MATCH

Mix and Match is one of the designer's explorations of 3D fashion. He wanted to put aside all the universal aesthetics of clothing, and create a unique or even crazy way of matching. At the same time, he omitted the facial features of all the characters because it could help people to focus on the clothing. To express personalities and emotions by clothing is something that the designer always wants to try. For him, the aim of clothing is not only to look good, but more importantly, to express one's inner world.

URIAL

AD & DS
Kevin Mikhail

2019

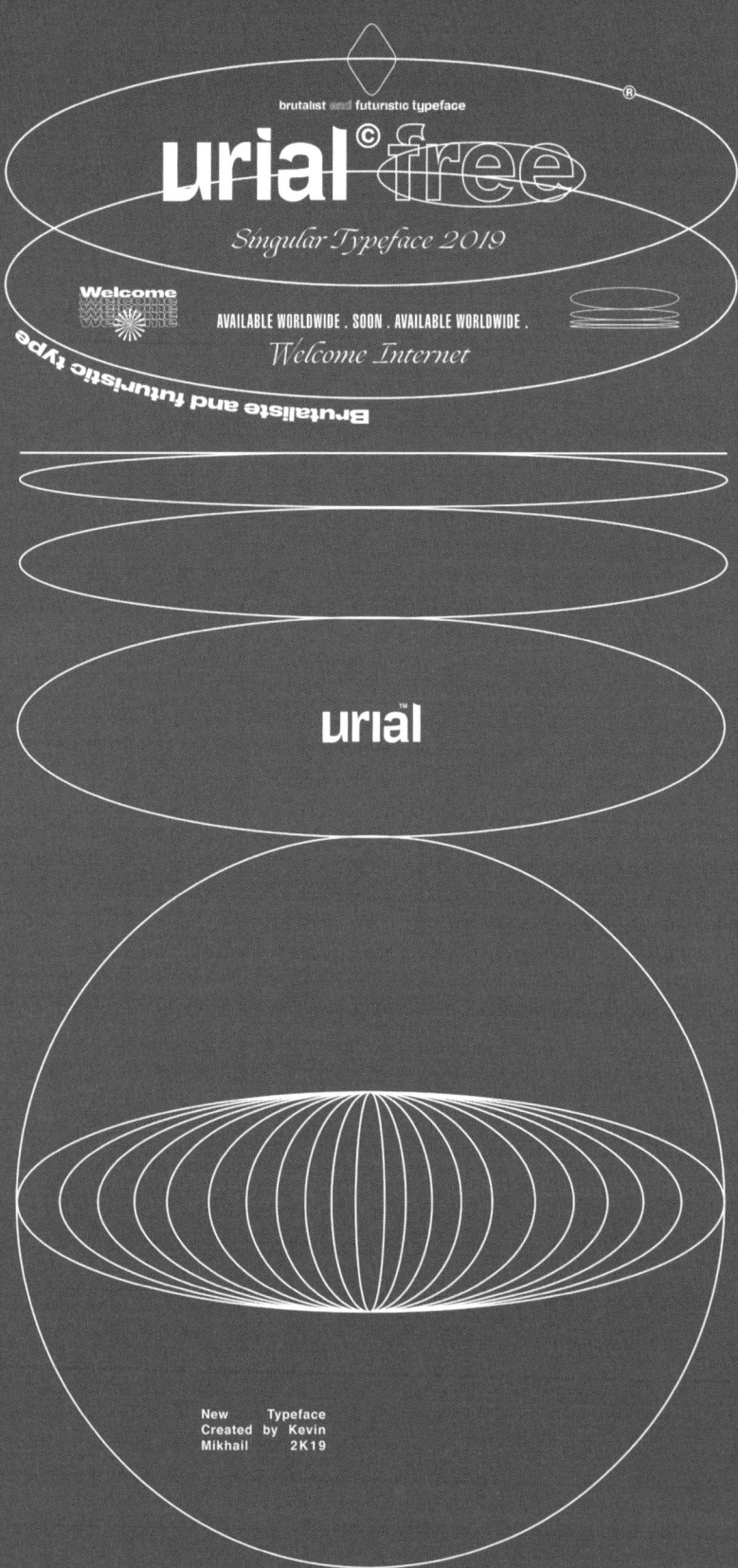

Urial reflects the current trend that values uniqueness and typographic recognisability. Typefaces no longer follow the same rules, they have become variable, alternative and have been modulated to the very limits of readability. Urial was designed to represent the contrast in the typefaces of this time. It is a balance between a very assertive character and a fundamentally readable typeface. This contemporary typeface is expressed by rounded cuts on the strokes that contrast with angular curls.

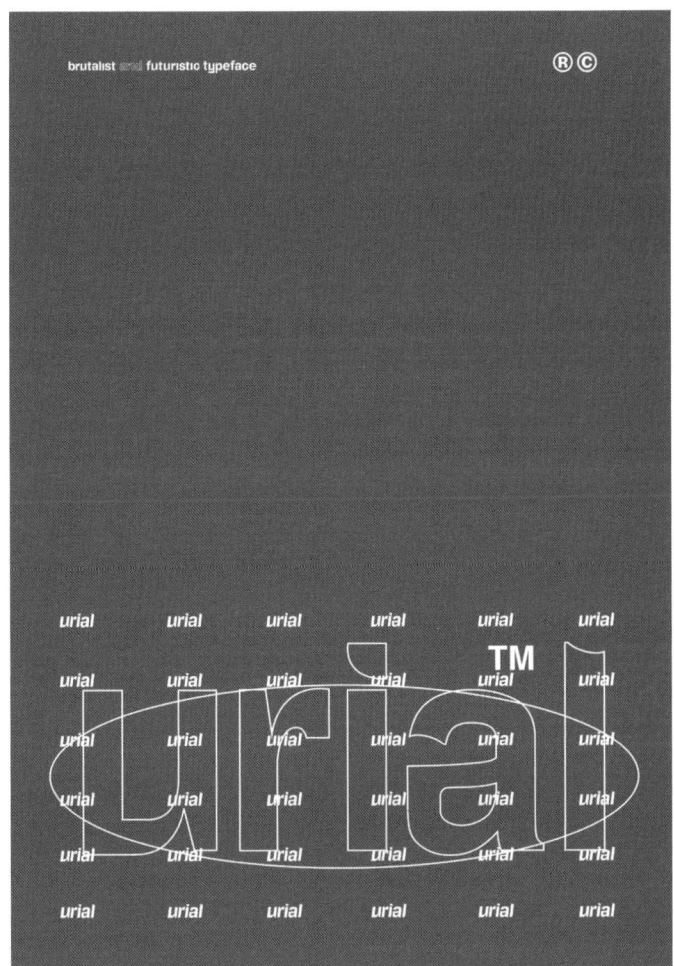
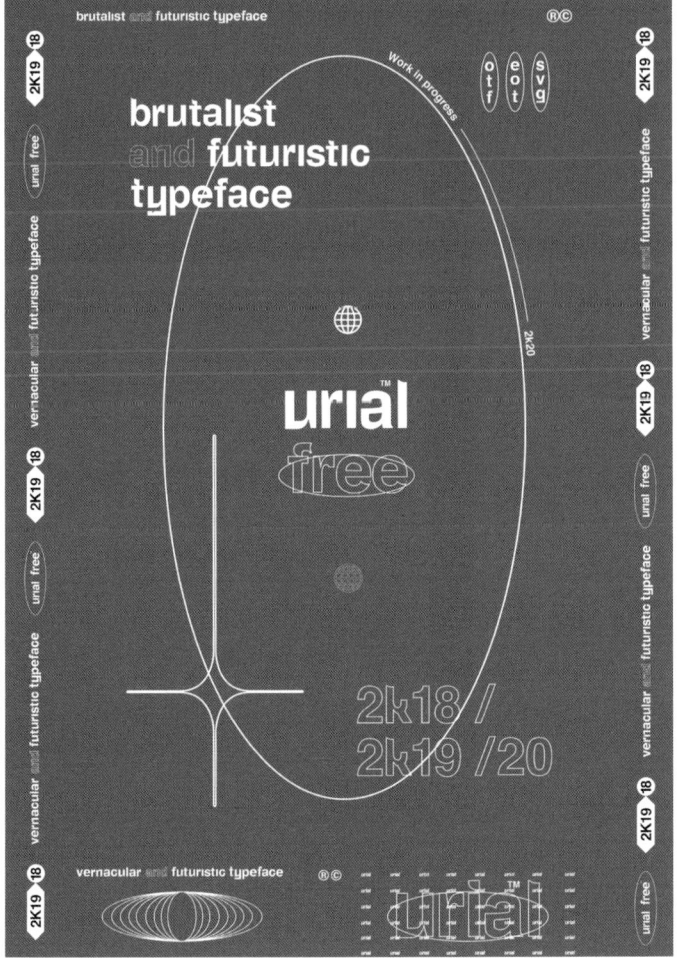

Published by **SendPoints IPS Co., Ltd** Publisher **Gengli Lin** Chief Editor **Nicole Lo** Design Director **Nicole Lo**
Designers **Yujie Lai & Yongqi Jian** Executive Editors **Gakky Luk, Wanting Wu & Luca Yin**
Editorial Desk *T: +86-20-89095121-8058*
E: editorial@brandmagazine.com.hk
Inquiry **Zebin Yao**
T: +86-20-89095121-8006
E: marketing@brandmagazine.com.hk (**Collaboration**)
ad@brandmagazine.com.hk (**Advertising**)
Sales Director **Philip Tsang**
T: +852-62962246
E: sales@sendpoints.cn
Address **Flat/Rm 4, 5/F, Tak Lee Building, 270-280 Queens Road West, Hong Kong**
T: +852-69502452
F: +852-35832448
E: info@brandmagazine.com.hk
Website **www.spbooks.cn**
ISSN **2226-6542**

International Distributors **UK**

Central Books
 T: +44-845-458-9925
 F: +44-845-458-9912
Arnolfini Books
 T: +44-117-9172306
 F: +44-117-9172303
Artwords Bookshop
 T: +44-20-7729-2000
 F: +44-20-7729-4400
Charlotte Street News
 T: +44-20-7636-4270
 F: +44-20-7419-7490
Fat Buddha Ltd
 T: +44-141-226-8972
Foyles
 T: +44-20-7440-3265

Centralbooks
 www.centralbooks.com
Newsstand
 www.newsstand.co.uk
Pineapple Media
 T: +44-23-9278-7970
 www.pineapple-media.com
ICA Bookshop
 T: +44-20-7930-3647
Germany
Do You Readme?! GbR [Berlin]
 T: +49-30-695-49-695
 F: +49-30-695-49-696
Amsterdam
Athenaeum Boekhandel
 T: +31-20-622-6248
 F: +31-20-638-4901

Poland
Muzeum Sztuki Nowoczesnej
  W Warszawie
  T: +48-501100882
Ireland
Books Upstairs
  T: +353-1-677-8566
Norway
Interpress Norge AS
  T: +47-225-73241
Portugal
In Uteis Design LDA [Lisbon]
  T: +351-225-088-474
  F: +351-225-088-475
Sweden
Svenska Interpress AB
  T: +46-8-506-506-00
USA
DisticorMagazine Distribution
Services
  T: +1-905-619-6565
Daily News
  T: +78111555
Chile
GONZALO OSORIO PETIT
  T: +56-32-2397498
  F: +56-32-2397498
Australia
Beautiful Pages
  T: +61-02-9356-2331
Mag Nation
  T: +61-03-9663-6559
Readings Pty Ltd
  T: +61-03-9347-6633

New Zealand
NATIONWIDE BOOK DISTRIBUTORS
  T: +64-3-312-1603
South Korea
Hong-ik Designbook
  T: +82-2-333-0342
Japan
TSUTAYA Books Daikanyama/T-SITE
  T: +81-3-3770-2525
TSUTAYA Books Roppongi
  T: +81-3-5775-1515
TSUTAYA Books Ginza
  T: +81-3-3575-7755
Singapore/Malaysia/Indonesia
Basheer Graphic
  T: +65-6336-0810
  T: +603-2713-2236
Thailand
Asia Books Co., Ltd
  T: +662-715-9000
India
SBD Subscription Services
  T: +91-11-2871-4138
China
SendPoints Books Co., Ltd [Mainland]
  T: +86-20-89095121-8038
Eslite Bookstore [Taiwan]
  T: +886-2-87893388 (Xinyi)
  T: +886-2-66365888 (Songyan)
Books.com.tw [Taiwan]
  T: +886-2-26535588
Eslite Bookstore [Hong Kong]
  T: +852-34196789 (Causeway Bay)
  T: +852-34191088 (Tsim Sha Tsui)
  T: +852-34191191 (Taikoo Shing)
  T: +852-31491035 (Olympic)
  T: +852-34191016 (Tuen Mun)

Typefaces: TheMix C4s, TheSans C4s, TheSerif HP, TheMixMono, TheSansMono (LucasFonts)
Contributions: We welcome all excellent relevant work contributions; however, we do reserve the right to select in accordance to different subject matters and quality purposes. All the works will be examined with respect and appreciation. The views expressed from all published works in *BranD* belong to the creators and do not represent *BranD*'s viewpoints.
Copyrights: All rights reserved. Reproduction in whole or in part without permission is strictly prohibited.
Special Thanks to: LucasFonts; Pimex, Cai Xing Jia (Paper)

©Steve Marchal—PP®F